M000105742

# NAVIGATING
# CHANGE

To Denys,
A warm of love +
presence —
with love + light!
Christine

# NAVIGATING
# CHANGE

## CONSCIOUS ENDINGS, VISIONARY BEGINNINGS

## CHRISTINE WARREN

FLAME
LANTERN
PRESS

SANTA FE

~

Names: Warren, Christine, 1951- author.

Title: Navigating change : conscious endings, visionary beginnings / Christine Warren.

Description: Santa Fe : Flame Lantern Press, [2017]

Identifiers: ISBN: 978-0-9991395-0-9 (paperback) | 978-0-9991395-1-6 (eBook) |
LCCN: 2017950525

Subjects: LCSH: Change. | Life change events. | Self-help techniques. | Attitude
change. | Life skills. | Conduct of life. | Self-realization. | Quality of life. | Success.
| Attitude (Psychology) | Self-actualization (Psychology) | Positive psychology. |
BISAC: SELF-HELP / Personal Growth / General. | BODY, MIND & SPIRIT
/ Inspiration & Personal Growth. | SELF-HELP / Motivational & Inspirational.

Classification: LCC: BF637.C4 W37 2017 | DDC: 158.1--dc23

FLAME LANTERN PRESS
Santa Fe

*This book is dedicated to
the thousands of extraordinary, inspiring,
courageous and loving people I've met in forty
years of teaching. Your stories, your journeys, and
your presence live on these pages.*

*And to my husband Kenn,
whose love is beyond words.*

# CONTENTS

# INTRODUCTION

When I was seven, my mother gave me a children's illustrated version of *The Pilgrim's Progress* by John Bunyan. Inside the endleaves of *The Pilgrim's Progress* was a hand drawn map I studied obsessively: the stages of change followed by the hero as he traveled through life. At the end of the path, I saw where our hero was headed: a beautiful castle high on a hill surrounded by light. I couldn't understand most of what I saw pictured on the map, but I knew it was very important. I believed that if I studied it enough, it would reveal a great secret.

I knew this book was onto a big truth. There was a map a person could follow in life to find the beautiful place, high on the hill, surrounded by light. As I read the tale, I could see on the map where our traveler was—here in the Slough of Despond or there in Vanity Fair. It encouraged me to know that, when he was hopelessly stuck in mud, helping beings showed up to lead him forward. It inspired me to know that, after getting lulled into sleepfullness in Vanity Fair, he'd wake up and spring forward on the map to find the kind Samaritan giving him comfort, bread, and food.

*This place where you are right now*
*God circled on a map for you . . .*
*Our Beloved has bowed there knowing*
*You were coming.*

≈⋆ HAFIZ

*Wherever you are is the
entry point.*

≋✣ KABIR

There's a secret place in us that wants to know where the hidden treasure is: that if we dig up the dirt, there's a glass jar with a message telling us our next step. If we crawl through the cave, we'll find a box with a key that will open the door at the back of the cave to let us out. If we climb higher in the tree to get a better perspective, we'll find the message we need dangling from a branch.

If we just know the map and follow it, we will get to the boon, the treasure, the gift. And in the magic of Old World tales, we're going to find out we had the treasure within us all along, only we couldn't find it without going through the map of change, step by step. We had the keys in our pockets all along: we were the ones we were searching for. Every step was perfect, even the painful ones, because they all deepened us, taught us, and led us back home, home to remember who we are.

This book, then, is your map for navigating change. It points out the pitfalls, it shows you how to climb out of the slough you are stuck in, how to cut through the forest of thorns surrounding you, how to find allies to guide you onward. It lets you know where you can get stuck, what to do if you land there, and how to extricate yourself. It reminds you always of the castle on the hill in the light that is your own Higher Self, always awaiting you through your journey through change.

Great, you're thinking, let's just cut a path straight to the castle. I wish we could do that, but most of us cannot springboard to the castle on the hill with the light around it. We need to walk the map and be instructed by the phases of change we go through in life. But the good news is that by knowing what the phases of change are, and finding out in this book how to move through your changes, you will gather courage, heart, and wisdom as you travel.

As you navigate your changes consciously, guided by this book, you'll find helping friends, messages in bottles, keys hidden in the dark caves, and lanterns shining in the dark nights. You'll get tools and helping skills. You'll hear tales of fellow journeyers and find out how they navigated their own trails upward and onward. As you follow the map, keep looking up, and remember where you are ultimately headed: back to your own true Being, living your own true expression.

This book is born of my own life experiences through many changes, and inspired by my work over several decades as a transformational teacher, coach, and counselor. I've worked with thousands of gifted, troubled, hopeful, despairing, extraordinary, and ordinary human beings, just like you and me, all of us trying to find our way home.

*Welcome to the path of change, friend.*
*The map is in your hands and the lantern is lit,*
*showing you the next steps to take. Read on, and*
*let's begin the journey.*

# The Four Phases of Navigating Change

**B**efore we begin our journey of change together, let's look at the territory we'll be travelling through, beginning with our endings and arriving at our new vision.

## PHASE 1

### Conscious Endings:
### Letting Go of the Old Form

*Begins on page 1*

## PHASE 4

### Visionary Beginnings:
### Creating From
### the Source

*Begins on page 161*

## PHASE 2

### The Mystery:
### Time to Retreat and
### Reflect

*Begins on page 69*

## PHASE 3

### The Phoenix Rises:
### Emergence of New Being

*Begins on page 111*

**In Phase 1, Conscious Endings,** you'll learn how to deeply integrate your past, finding healing, power, and hope as you move forward. ❧ You'll become aware of why you made former choices, what's changed for you now, and who you have become. ❧ You'll find gratitude for what served you and was truly good in your past. ❧ You'll learn how to forgive others, both humanly and spiritually, finding authentic integration and peace. ❧ You'll empower yourself with the lessons and wisdom you have gained.

**Phase 2, The Mystery,** guides you through the germinal time between forms when you can't see what's next. ❧ You'll learn how to turn feelings of chaos and confusion into clarity and trust. ❧ You'll learn how to create or deepen your meditation practice to help you attune to Spirit. ❧ You'll embrace this time to retreat and reflect as a profound gift that brings you deep insights and new direction for your journey.

**In Phase 3, The Phoenix Rises,** you'll discover a new way of Being emerging out of your passage through Phases 1 and 2. ❧ You'll create a powerful Being Vision, a personal credo by which you'll measure all possible paths and choices. You'll discover the intrinsic joy that comes from living sourced by Being, which ultimately leads you to creating your new life vision.

**In Phase 4, Visionary Beginnings,** you'll learn a powerful new way to manifest your next expression, informed by the illuminating teachings of quantum physics and metaphysics. ❧ You'll be guided in creating your next vision, and learn how to take action led by your Higher Self. ❧ You'll hear inspiring stories of others who initiated new visions using these principles. ❧ You'll take flight into the next chapters of your life, born from the gifts you've gathered through all four phases of change.

# How to Journey
# with this Book

1 ✍ **COMMIT TO THE JOURNEY AND FOLLOW THE PLAN.**
The plan works! Over a thousand people going
through major life shifts have taken my "Navigating
Change" workshops, and nearly all have experienced
profound shifts and breakthroughs. They learned and
practiced the same exercises and teachings you'll find
within these pages.

2 ✍ **READ THE BOOK SEQUENTIALLY, DOING THE EXER-
CISES AND PRACTICES AS YOU COME TO THEM.** Think of
this book as your friend, walking the trail through your
change with you, giving you inspiration, guidance, and
support. The teachings, practices, and stories are created
in a step-by-step journey to help you integrate your
past, rest in not-knowing, find who you are becoming,
and then discover your next outer expression.

3 ✍ **FEEL FREE TO FLIP THESE PAGES OPEN FOR SPON-
TANEOUS INSIGHTS AND INSPIRATION.** Change is an
organic process, and you may be working with different phases of change simultaneously in different ways.
Skip around through these pages or open this book
randomly for inspiration. You might ask a question,
open the book spontaneously, and see what shows up
for you. Use it to guide and inspire yourself.

4 ✍ **START A CHANGE JOURNAL.** Buy yourself a special change journal and keep it at hand as you read,

doing the exercises and, if you like, drawing pictures or symbols depicting your inner work. This enlivens and personalizes the lessons and benefits of each phase. Go back and reread what you've written or drawn. Read it out loud. Read it to a trusted friend, so you can really hear yourself—your truth, your *ahas*, your personal insights. Journaling leads us from where we are now to our deepest truths. Let your pen be your guide.

5 🖙 **BE FULLY HUMAN AND FULLY DIVINE.** True spiritual teaching embraces both our humanity and our divinity. I am a firm believer in being authentically real and human, while remembering who we are as beings connected to a higher power, or Spirit. You'll find specific ways to move through the nitty-gritty fears and feelings that are part of all major life shifts. You'll also be reminded that you are bigger than your present challenges and troubles. You are an extension of Spirit, a part of God, and you have constant access to your own Higher Self, always ready to take your hand and show you the way forward.

6 🖙 **REMEMBER THAT THE CHANGE JOURNEY IS ALWAYS REPEATING ITSELF, KEEPING YOUR LIFE EVOLVING, EXPANDING, AND CREATIVE.** As you outgrow old forms in your life, or let go of old ways of being, you will move through these phases again, but each time at a higher level than before. Allow the gifts of change to deepen and expand you to grow into your fullest personal and spiritual potentials.

## *Let's begin!*

# PHASE 1

# CONSCIOUS ENDINGS

*Letting Go of
the Old Form*

# PHASE 1

꧁

# Conscious Endings:
# Letting Go of the Old Form

Welcome to your journey of navigating change. You are in a sacred transition, a potent time where your old ways of knowing yourself and living your life are in transformation. Things in your life may be falling away, relationships may be in shift, work you identified with may be no longer right for you, or no longer available to you. Your boat has cast off from the harbor and you are looking out to sea, wondering where you're travelling and what's ahead. You are exactly where you should be right now, even though it may feel chaotic or overwhelming at times. Let's walk together through these pages as you navigate your life change.

Phase 1, "Conscious Endings," initiates your journey. These pages will guide you through the completion of your past and the integration of the situation, relationship, or way of Being in your life that is now coming to a close. In Phase 1, you'll take time to honor who and what has been present in your life. You'll discover what you've learned thus far, gathering your power and wisdom from all you've experienced. You'll find the liberation of authentic forgiveness.

There is a new possibility for your life calling. The teachings, practices, and stories found in this phase help you find

*I have always known that at last I would take this road, but yesterday, I did not know that it would be today.*

꧁ NARIHARA

strength, healing, and vision as you move forward. Integrating your endings well gives you hope, peace of mind, self-esteem, and deep closure with what you are moving on from and prepares you for what lies ahead.

## Phase 1: Conscious Endings includes:

# Change as a Sacred
# Time of Initiation

## Freeing the Angel Within

**The change you are going through right now in your life is a time of initiation into a new way of living your life.** The purpose of this change is to awaken you to your true Being, the part of you who is connected at the Source to Spirit. To embody that truth, what does not fit has to be removed so the angel of yourself can emerge. The removal of what no longer fits your big Self has catalyzed this change in your life. You are in an initiatory journey, releasing what no longer serves you to become the angel of your true Self.

We must let life chisel away who we used to be and the forms we once put in place that reflected our old selves. Whether you personally initiated leaving a form that no longer served you, or whether life has taken away a marriage, friend, job, home, or other form you thought you needed to be whole, you are in a time of sacred initiation.

*I saw the angel in the marble and carved until I set him free.*

≈✦ MICHELANGELO

You are being sculpted with love and clarity by the kind hand of the great Creator. It's time to embrace the process of change and transformation, and let your inner sculptor reveal the angel.

To create a new life, we must consciously let go of the old. This is the sacred initiation work of life change. In every initiatory ritual throughout world cultures, the initiate must release a part of his or her former identity in order to open up to a new, larger sense of self.

## Who's Dying? Who's Being Born? Relinquishing Your Old Identity

*We need to take time in our own underground to let go of the past, in order to move forward with a truly new self-identity.* I learned about this once on a horseback ride with the grandson of a tribal elder in New Mexico. As the two of us rode through his ancestral lands, he spontaneously shared about his coming-of-age initiation into the tribe. As a teacher of change and transformation, I was honored and grateful to receive such extraordinary information.

We ambled along a mesa on dusty Indian ponies, and he spoke of his initiation into manhood. He shared that 13-year-old boys are separated for one year from their mothers and live together in an underground kiva (a large, dugout room carved into the earth, and held as sacred), where they are attended to and instructed by the men of the tribe. For this year they cannot see their mothers at all, in order to break off from being boys and step into their manhood. They only eat foods grown in the earth. They have to give up pizza, sodas, chips, and all the processed

*We must be willing to let go of the life we have planned, so as to find the life that is waiting for us.*

⇒ JOSEPH CAMPBELL

food teenagers usually love. At the end of this intensive year, they are embraced ritually by the entire community as men and step into their new role as men of the tribe.

Our indigenous brothers and sisters understand that life calls for a time of letting go, going underground, and sacrificing old ways of being, in order to take on a new identity. This young man's elders knew that a period of letting go of old, outgrown identities was essential for boys to become men. We may judge the severity of their rituals through our Western eyes, but the resulting sense of belonging, community value, and place in their tribal community is enviable to those of us who grew up disconnected from ceremony and acknowledgement of our life transitions.

Lacking understanding about the sacred nature of life change, it is no wonder that when forms are dissolving in our lives, we think something is out of whack. We struggle, go into denial, or push forward too fast to create new relationships, jobs, or homes. Once in our new forms of life, we may wonder why we feel unhappy, depressed, and unfulfilled. In not taking time to *be* with our endings and to honor our letting go, we may eventually see that we have simply recreated who we used to be in another package.

What old identity in you is dying right now? Who is being born? Breathe deeply, allow your own letting-go time to be a period of initiation preparing you for your future, and give yourself to it. At the end will come the next chapter of your life, and you will truly be ready for it.

*. . . life calls for a time of letting go, going underground, and sacrificing old ways of being, in order to take on a new identity.*

# Collecting Your Gold: Getting the Gifts from the Past

## Tracking the Past: Who Was I Then?

*Those who ignore history are bound to repeat it.*

*≈ GEORGE SANTAYANA*

*In conscious endings, we are tracking our pasts to see who we used to be and recognize the part of us who chose our now-outgrown forms.* Our past tracking helps us follow the trail from who we once were to who we are now. We see why we made our past choices, and understand why things changed as we've changed. We become detectives of our own journeys, asking, "Who was I then? Why did I once choose this form? What were my old values, needs, or unhealed places from which I made this choice?"

In one of my early past trackings, I followed my own trail of leaving university a year before graduating to join Twin Oaks, an intentional farming community of fifty people in Virginia. Who was I then? I had an unstable childhood with constant moving, much loneliness, new schools almost yearly, and a fractured home life. I never felt I belonged anywhere. At twenty, I desperately needed roots, stability, and belonging. I dreamed of having a joyful, caring family who loved me. In my dream, I lived on a farm with cats and cows, barns and gardens, chickens and apple trees. I would never move. There would be no violence, little conflict, and music, country life, and lots of hugs. I would be a treasured member of this family. Always the new girl in school, lonely and trying to fit into long-established cliques, I at last would belong somewhere wonderful.

At Twin Oaks, I found the home of my dreams. I discovered bear hugs and laughter, music and creativity and farm life, big homemade meals, cows strolling in the pastures, swimming together in the South Anna River after a day's work in the fields. I found a welcoming tribe of caring, good souls living an Arcadian dream. When I applied for membership, I was invited to join right away. That was it: I was hooked, wanted, chosen. Degrees and university life seemed meaningless—after all, in the idealism of the young, I was going to live at Twin Oaks forever.

For the first time in my life, I had a big, stable family and was really wanted and loved. The yet-unhealed wounds of my childhood made this more important than getting a degree or establishing myself in a career. Living communally and doing fifty work hours a week on the farm was far more instructive in the art of living than several years in a university had been.

When I finally left Twin Oaks, it was to join yet another community. I wanted a spiritual lifestyle and teacher. I wanted to keep living in a big, loving community, but one with a committed spiritual focus and lifestyle. I joined Kripalu Yoga Ashram\*, a community of thirty-five members, and remained there for thirteen years.

*\*Now Kripalu Center, a large program center in Stockbridge, Massachusetts, and no longer an ashram.*

After fifteen years in intentional communities, at thirty-five I had fulfilled my need for family and belonging in a community form. The form once so perfect for me had become like a too-tight coat that I needed to discard. I was no longer that young, insecure woman seeking family and belonging. I had healed and grown. New chapters were calling, and I said yes to them.

As you track your past, ask yourself: Who *was* that man or woman in me who chose that career, that marriage, that path? How have I changed and grown, so that now something new is being called forth in my life? In seeing the perfection of your past choices, you are ready to shed one more layer to let the new life come through.

## Pulling Back the Camera: Your Soul Curriculum

*As souls, we choose the life experiences that will best teach us what we need to learn.* In describing a difficult work experience that was catalyzing old painful patterns, my client Ricardo, a PBS writer and producer, once said, "Christine, I'm pulling back the camera," to get a bigger perspective on the lessons that were presenting themselves to him through his situation. I loved this image.

The intensity and turbulence we can feel when navigating big life changes can cause us to become myopic, preoccupied with the seeming unfairness or difficulty of our situations. We need to pull back the camera from the immediate drama of our situations to see how this life change is teaching us, playing a perfect part in our soul curriculum.

Your soul curriculum is what you are here to learn in this life, your life major. Some of us are here to learn forgiveness, or empowerment, or compassion, or self-esteem.

You can see your major, the lessons your soul is here to learn, by witnessing your life experiences. When you learn your soul lessons and integrate this wisdom, you graduate and move on. When that happens, these old experiences either cease to occur, or just flow past you without disturbing your peace. You come to recognize the remaining lessons coming in and say, "Oh, you again," even with humor.

*Life experiences do not automatically teach us.*

However, life experiences do not automatically teach us. We have the choice to walk through life blaming others and feeling victimized, or to use all that occurs to awaken and grow. The choice is ours. We make empowered choices to use our circumstances to evolve when we embrace change consciously as a perfect opportunity to learn and change ourselves positively through our presenting predicaments.

When you pull back your inner camera and regard your whole life in this evolutionary perspective, you can view betrayals, hurts, losses, and failures in their perfection, as perfect classes for your learning. You are not a billiard ball bouncing around the table of life, smacked by this person, that betrayal, this loss, that disappointment, hoping you don't fall permanently into a hole of failure and pain. You are a great soul! You are expanding in your wisdom and love to fulfill your purpose in being on the planet. Everything is right on track for your soul curriculum.

## Sudden Disappointments: Blessings in Disguise

**Have heart when you are rejected or a form you love leaves your life experience against your conscious wishes.** The sweeping changes in our lives that initiate new identities, new visions, and profound transformations are not always initiated by us. When someone else rejects us or something we loved—a home, a job, a place—is no more a part of our lives, we can suffer profound pain and sudden disappointment. But often what appears to be a disturbing loss of love, home, career, or belonging becomes the perfect gift for our growth.

One autumn morning in 2006, I was meditating over morning tea in my garden, sitting in the shade of the apple-loaded branches of my favorite tree. A longtime mentoring relationship in my life that I treasured had recently morphed into personal friendship, initiated by my mentor. I asked Spirit for guidance about this friendship, one that seemed to promise a closeness that my remaining childhood wounds longed for. Beware the attractions to situations and people who appear to give us what we crave, while making us go blind to the inherent shadows!

I turned to my collection of Rumi poetry and asked to be guided to a poem that would instruct me. My book fell open to the poem "Sudden Disappointments." How prophetic the guidance of this moment actually was revealed itself painfully in the months to come. This so-called friendship crashed and burned, evoking my deepest unhealed wounds about women and friendships, and dragging me into the underground to find strength and healing on my own.

In the poem I had turned to, Rumi tells of an eagle snatching up the Prophet Mohammed's boot when he removed his shoes to kneel in prayer. As Mohammed watched, the eagle

> ☙
>
> *. . . Learn from this eagle story*
>
> *That when misfortune comes,*
> *you must quickly praise.*
>
> *Others may be saying, Oh no, but you*
>
> *Will be opening out like a rose*
>
> *Losing itself petal by petal.*
>
> *Don't grieve for what doesn't come.*
>
> *Some things that don't happen*
>
> *Keep disasters from happening.*
>
> ☙ RUMI, *"Joy at Sudden Disappointment"**

*The Essential Rumi, trans. by Coleman Barks

flew to the sky and upturned the boot, and a poisonous snake fell out.

What had appeared to be a disturbing loss actually saved his life. The poem ends with Rumi's marvelous teachings of trusting the Divine plan of Spirit always governing our lives.

This poem was a direct dart of spiritual guidance, going straight to the bull's eye heart-center of what I needed to heal in myself. It predicted accurately what this friendship's ending would bring to me over the ensuing months—painful disappointment, apparent loss, and, ultimately, finding deep personal empowerment and liberation in my own heart. I indeed had to stop seeking love outside of myself in this burgeoning intimate friendship that promised much, and instead discover it everywhere around me.

Another's rejection, a lover or spouse leaving you, a friend ending contact, a beloved or needed job evaporating, a treasured home no longer being yours, all hurl you into the fires of change whether you thought you wanted to cook there or not. Yet the Universe has its eye on your soul curriculum at all times. Sweeping losses that come as shocks have a purpose in helping you grow and deepen and expand.

*Remember that you are in the hands of the great loving, guiding Spirit.*

Remember that you are in the hands of the great loving, guiding Spirit. If you work with your loss and change consciously, over time you will see clearly how your apparent loss was a gift in your life. With the passage of time and conscious attention to your inner process, you will look back at this event, which once seemed to be an error in the big plan for your life, and feel gratitude and awe at God's map directing you forward. You will see where you have gone and who you have become through this change.

The choice to get the gold from the past is in your hands. Such gratitude and joyful reflection do not automatically happen. Some people choose to spend their lives in regret, bitterness, or desolation over apparent endings that were initiated by forces or persons outside of themselves. Don't be one of these. The spiritually embraced loss, in time, becomes a golden doorway to your future. At the right moment, when you have done your inner work and are ready, you will walk through that doorway into your own expansive new Being, as described in Phase 3, "The Phoenix Rises: Emergence of New Being."

# Heeding the Call for Change

## Taking Off the Old Coat: When What Once Nurtured You Now Constricts You

**W**e are meant to evolve and change, and as we do, we outgrow many of the forms that once served us. I was hanging out with my old friend Thomas Amelio after leading a workshop at Kripalu Center. We had grown up together in the ashram, sharing over thirty years of metaphysical friendship. Thomas peered at me closely. "Christine, isn't it time for you to leave your corporate training career?" he asked bluntly. "I mean, don't you want work that is aligned to the big soul you are? It's like a tight coat that's suffocating you. You need to get out." I liked his bluntness, felt seen and loved by it. He was right.

We are evolutionary beings, here to grow and change. As we leave the old forms we created of marriage, relationships, careers, life situations and ways of Being, it's like taking off an old, familiar coat that once suited us perfectly but is now too tight, binding us from free movement.

*Most men lead lives of quiet desperation.*

⇒❋ HENRY DAVID THOREAU, *Walden*

We are not meant to live static lives of predictability, not here to establish the perfect partnerships, homes, and careers, and then sit quietly by, unchanging in our dance of life as the years roll on. We chose the past forms in our lives predicated on who we were then and what we needed. Those past choices made perfect sense when we made them, aligned to the still-unhealed wounds that drove our values and longings at that time, and a perfect match for the needs and perceptions we had of what would be the perfect marriage, job, or place to live, the perfect life. When we have completed what we needed in those old forms, change stands up and shakes herself off like a wet dog saying, "That was a good swim. What's next?"

To live from our big aliveness and joy, we must hear and follow the call of the soul asking for change and alignment to our bigger purpose. Denial of our call for a new way of inhabiting life can lead to chronic depression, overeating, or abuse of substances and alcohol, or else to a deadening of the spirit as we try to numb ourselves against the tides of change washing over us. Our lives could become, as Thoreau said, "lives of quiet desperation," as we deny our real needs and shrink ourselves to fit into the old coats of our past. But even our desperation, if embraced and worked with consciously, becomes an opening door to positive change and growth. In the disintegration of the old, a new way of living life is waiting to be born.

What tight old coats are you still wearing? Name them. Thank them for keeping you warm. And consider taking them off so the new you can step forth.

*. . . even our desperation, if embraced and worked with consciously, becomes an opening door to positive change and growth.*

## Disintegration Precedes Reintegration

***The disintegration of the old precedes a new integration in your life.*** The unraveling at times of the old forms in your life and identity is critical if you are to live a life of purpose and passion. There can be no new life without releasing the outgrown parts of the life you once wanted.

Although times of disintegration can feel scary, have faith: you're on the right path. Psychic space must be opened up for your new life to have breathing space. You cannot hold on to the outgrown structures of your past and still create space for what is trying to come in. By allowing time for the disintegration of what your life used to look like, your joyful new vision can find room to reach you.

Endings and disintegration are part of the natural cycle of life. Watch nature in her deep earth wisdom. As the leaves fall to the ground, they disintegrate. The flower petals and fruits that preceded the leaves have also fallen and disintegrated, lost their once beautiful wholeness. But in the drying, crumbling leaves, the rotted fruit and fallen seeds on the ground, new life is germinating in winter's rest. With time, new trees, plants, and new life will burst forth.

Nature teaches us the way of all things. We too must allow the timely dropping away of old forms in their natural cycles and a time of germination and rest in order for our new visions to come forth, nurtured and fertilized by what fell away. All is in place, and all is as it should be. Have trust in the endings, and know that a new integration is waiting around the corner to enhance your big full life.

*And the day came when the risk to remain tight in a bud was more painful than the risk it took to blossom.*

≈ ANAÏS NIN

## When We Won't Let Go of an Outgrown Form, It Often Lets Us Go

**Sometimes we cling to a job, relationship, place, or situation in our lives out of insecurity or habit, even when it is no longer aligned to the bigger person we have become.**

*You've seen my descent.*
*Now watch my rising.*

≈✲ RUMI

Julie joined my Santa Fe women's group after moving to town following the ending of her forty-year marriage. Her life had been devoted to her family. One day her husband announced that he was in love with his young secretary and was ending the marriage. The entire fabric of her life split open, leaving her in free fall without a net.

But life had gifts waiting for Julie in this apparent forced ending, one long overdue for her merry soul. She left the provincial town in New Mexico where they had lived and bought a home in Santa Fe, a bold move. Although she had never joined a spiritual or personal growth group in her life, she called to participate in my women's group. Julie became a treasured regular group member. The group witnessed her healing of her past and initiating of her new life as the seasons flowed by.

In Santa Fe, although single and living alone at sixty for the first time in her life, Julie found herself. She shared with us about her journey to heal her past and envision a new future for herself. She found a tough inner strength and a powerful voice in standing up for her financial rights in the divorce settlement, a process that took three years of steady, unrelenting negotiation as she refused to be minimized financially. She did shamanic healing with a local practitioner. She took a gastronomic tour of France, cooking in villages with master chefs and attending group dinners in a sexy new black dress bought for the trip. She pushed herself into new experiences and discovered new parts of herself at every turn.

In our groups, Julie took risks and broke new ground in relating and expressing herself. As three years passed, I saw her transform from a quiet Midwestern woman, transplanted to New Mexico as a young wife, and unsure of her voice, to a deep, fun, dynamic woman exploring her life with gusto. Her radiant woman stepped forward. She actually became more physically beautiful as time progressed, sparkling and luminous.

Although the harsh ending in her life had been a massive adjustment, her integration of her ending process gave birth to a new woman of vitality. In our last group, Julie declared, "My divorce has really been the greatest gift of my life—the best thing that ever happened to me." The group broke into applause.

Old wounds and outgrown emotional needs of the past can keep us hanging on to people or situations we thought we needed, but which are no longer right for who we've evolved to be. If we cling to someone or something out of outgrown self-concepts, and we don't let go when we should, sometimes life kicks our butts and breaks the relationships or situations off through the others' rejection.

With our inner truth-gathering and the wisdom of hindsight, we are likely to look back and realize how rejections or endings thrust upon us were the greatest gift to our development and growth.

## Living the Life You Want: Your Life as Art

***This is your life, your canvas to paint upon. What will you leave behind, and what will you create there?*** You have the right to live as fulfilling and creative a live as you can allow yourself to. There are no limits, except those you place on yourself in your thinking. But you yourself must make the choice to paint on your own life canvas with the colors you choose. No one can make you, and no one can stop you.

Your life is in your hands. You are never stuck in a form you once created unless you allow yourself to be stuck. But we sometimes learn, as I did, by allowing ourselves to be

*Life is a great big canvas. Throw all the paint on it you can.*

≡✦ DANNY KAYE

stuck in places and forms not aligned to our greatest good, and giving away our power to live as we choose.

Early on in my post-ashram career as a corporate trainer, I had lunch with Dale, an art therapist friend who is also a painter. Dale shared that she took Mondays off to paint in her home studio. So wondrous and impossible did this seem to me at the time that I felt like she had said, "Oh yes, I fly to the moon and back every Monday." I responded wistfully, "Oh God, I would love to do that," as if this were tantamount to breaking a cardinal rule of life: Thou Shalt Not Take Mondays Off to Follow Your Bliss. Stellar moments that impact us often remain imprinted in memory, and this was such a moment. Dale gazed into my eyes and said, "Christine, you have the right to live the life you want to live." Really?

*. . . you have the right to live the life you want to live.*

Living the life I dreamed of living—what a concept! A Fine Arts Major in college and lifetime painter and creative being, in the previous few years I had lost touch with my big sense of self-determination to follow my own true path. My spiritual training in the ashram, so full of deep value, had its shadow side as well.

Living thirteen years in the ashram was a gift that has shaped who I am in positive ways. I found the teacher inside me in those years, and she bloomed and flourished within the ashram's hothouse environment of personal growth, deep mentoring, and spiritual training. The calling to share what I have learned as a teacher was also an archetypal part of me, having always been part of my childhood play with the neighborhood kids. But I lost the feisty, independent artist within me, although I did manage to wedge her into my packed schedule.

My ashram soul-dilemma was that, in practicing surrendering my ego and its desires—lofty work for a young woman in her twenties—I had completely lost touch with my own strong vision for my life. I no longer took my own dreams and longings seriously, influenced by years in the ashram of ignoring them as shallow fantasies, less important than my great spiritual ideals.

I later realized we cannot give up egos we've not yet developed, and that pursuing our human dreams is integral to our soul-purpose for being embodied on earth. Uplifting, illuminating people are those who live uplifting, visionary lives and follow their own stars, wherever they lead them. Through losing touch with myself and my true vision, I had become temporarily deadened to my own longings and passions.

When I married and moved out of the ashram, I made the classic navigating change blunder that I now teach about: I changed the outer form of my life, but not who I truly was inside of it. I slid into a career offered me as a corporate and leadership trainer, one for which my teaching experience suited me perfectly. I did not know who I was and what I wanted. I lacked the wisdom contained in this book: to take time to integrate the powerful ashram past I was leaving and to rest awhile in the Mystery before lunging forward into a new career. As everything serves our souls' growth, in a universal sense it was all perfect. But you may save yourself a decade or more by reading on . . .

## Getting What We Thought We Wanted: The Trap of Success

In my new career as an executive team builder and trainer, my closet became schizophrenic. One half was elegant corporate attire and the scarves, heels, silk blouses, and

*Uplifting, illuminating people are those who live uplifting, visionary lives and follow their own stars, wherever they lead them.*

*Beware of all enterprises requiring new clothes.*

☞ HENRY DAVID THOREAU, *Walden*

briefcase that went with them. The other half was my flowered gypsy dresses, long skirts, jeans, denim shirts, and hip clothing, the trappings of my "real" self. I sometimes wondered what would happen if I met a corporate client on the street in my own clothes, so split were my career world and personal self into these two aberrant dimensions.

I was in a success trap resulting from not having taken time to be clear about my own vision for my life and work before plunging into a new career. It was a trap of my own making, one I was solely responsible for. I had become successful in a world that was not the one I wanted. It was never my personal dream to work in high-end, urban, corporate buildings in elegant suits, being successful with corporate executives, facilitating meetings in elegant resorts or in polished Manhattan boardrooms. I was living someone else's success fantasy.

I found a measure of happiness and fulfillment for a time. I travelled to some exotic places and met many wonderful human beings among my clientele in those years, some of whom became personal friends. Our clients loved the services my partner and I offered. My income surpassed my wildest ashram dreams, which was not a difficult feat.

But I was not living my own authentic life. Early in my new career, I lived in Reykjavik for many months while serving several leading corporations there. When not on the job, I sat on street corners like a college kid, drawing and painting the romantic old rooftops and gables of the charming Icelandic buildings. After training trips, I rushed home to Massachusetts to get into jeans and paint all weekend with music playing, so happy to be back with my creative artist-self.

A shattering moment of truth occurred for me when the owner of one of Iceland's largest corporations, a wonderful

*Which causes more suffering: success or failure?*

≋ LAO TZU,
*Tao Te Ching*

man who was my client, kindly came to the airport to see my partner and me off following our work with his company. We sat over coffee in the airport lounge. He turned to me and said, "You must love what you do." It was a horrible moment of feeling completely split. I *did* love this man and his team, with whom we'd spent four days' training at his country house, helping them align some major challenges in their relationships, vision, and company. But, at that moment, I knew inside myself that I was leading a double life. I was not leading my authentic life. I was cramming my artistic soul like tissue paper around the solid gift to others of my corporate training. I intuitively felt I could become seriously ill if I continued to carry such a deep split in my life. Something had to give.

## Following Your Truth

**Only you can give up your power to lead the life of your dreams, and only you can take it back.** You alone can make the empowered choice to follow your own bliss. You do not need anyone's permission. The power to choose is yours. In the end, I had to follow my call to live my own life, living each day from my own vision. I could no longer give up the creative, more spacious life that was calling me. I wanted to paint fulltime, not just on weekends and on vacation. I was willing to give up my big house in the country and simplify my material life to follow my truth.

After deep therapeutic exploration, reams of journaling, and earnest prayers, I made the decision to move to Santa Fe and paint fulltime. As I left the corporate world, the glue that held my marriage in place as creative business partners dried up. My first husband and I had grown apart

*Far better to live your own path imperfectly than to live another's perfectly.*

❀ The Bhagavad Gita

in our lifestyle values, though we shared humor, affection, and respect. We decided to separate.

I withdrew for a time and went on a retreat in the New Mexican desert, a time in the Mystery. I wanted space to dwell on my entire life, the path I had travelled, my ten-year marriage, my unfulfilled longings. I retreated to a remote meditation center in the Manzano Mountains owned by Peter and Linda, two beloved friends. The center was empty except for the three of us. I had complete freedom to be alone, to feel all my feelings, explore every angle of my change, and make sure that I was doing the right thing in leaving my marriage and moving west, essentially changing my entire life. The desert light and silence showed me that I was. In Phase 2, "The Mystery," in this book, I describe that inner time and how I used it.

I moved to Santa Fe shortly after this. I had my divorce settlement and modest savings, enough to live simply while painting for a couple of years. My first day in town I found an old adobe guesthouse on Canyon Road, with three kiva fireplaces and a small walled garden of fruit trees and red poppies. I moved there with books, art supplies, and my cat, Zoë. For seven years I painted fulltime, was eventually invited to show in a gallery, took part in group shows, and sold a respectable amount of work, though sales were not my primary motive. I finally completely lived my lifetime artist-dream. I put my suits in mothballs.

My wildly changed new life revolved around morning meditation in the hot sunshine of Santa Fe, painting for hours, journaling over a latte late afternoons in my favorite outdoor coffee bar, something I had rarely had time for in my previous life. I thrived. I fell in love with a beautiful man, Kenn, who is now my husband. We had little money in our early years together, but I felt rich.

At the end of my last one-person show, seven years after my relocation west, I had completed my longing to be a professional painter. I no longer felt the desire to paint fulltime, produce the landscapes clients wanted, and show publicly. I was ready to return to my deeper lifetime calling of being a transformational teacher. I had followed my old artist-calling, and it was all good. I felt whole, I was done. It was again time for another major change.

# Making Right Decisions: When to Stay and When to Go

## What Question Is Your Soul Asking Now?

*Always the beautiful answer who asks a beautiful question.*

≋✲ e.e. cummings

*If you are in a great life transition, your soul is on the phone, and it has a question to ask you. What is the question being asked of you right now by your soul?*

To answer this question you must temporarily set aside concerns about outer forms, such as: Should I quit my job? Should I move here or there? Should I be in relationship with this person or not? Should I follow this new direction in life or stay where I am? Being prematurely engaged in these outer issues distracts you from your soul questions: Who am I now? How did I get here? How have I changed?

Before you initiate big outer change, begin by hearing and answering your soul's questions. Take creative, meditative space in your life to listen to your soul, hear the real question being asked, and find your authentic answer.

## Ask Yourself the Right Question

An example of finding the soul question took place in one of my "Navigating Change" workshops. Annie sat in the back of the room, tears streaming down her face. She waved her hand to speak, pregnant with a deep question.

"Yes?"

"Christine, I have to make a decision. I feel that I want to leave my marriage. After twenty-seven years, two grown children, and my daughter's wedding coming up in nine months, and her begging me not to leave my husband and ruin her wedding, I have to make a huge decision. And I don't know how to make it."

"What's the decision?"

"I have to decide whether to stay with my husband, or leave him."

"No, that's not the decision you have to make," I said, as forty faces looked at me curiously, as if to say, *"It's not?"* A bit of a ham, I admit I enjoyed this moment of high drama.

"The decision you have to make," I said, "is this: *Who do you want to be? How do you want to live? What is your vision for your life now?* When you know what you want, and who you want to be, and how you wish to live, then you have the option to explore your vision with your husband to see if you can evolve together in this marriage. I recommend giving that some care and time after spending twenty-seven years together. Give him an opportunity to meet the emerging woman in you and see if you and he

*Your real decision to walk forward with vision on your true path, and to live from your highest values and Self, or to remain in old patterns that you have outgrown.*

can work things out in this old form. He may surprise you. He also might want no part of the woman you are becoming now. It might threaten him. He simply may not want to change. He may want you to stay as you were.

"Your real decision is not about leaving or not leaving your husband. It's a choice whether to embrace the new woman in you who is seeking bigger life expression. It's a decision to walk forward with vision on your true path, to live from your highest values and Self, or to remain in old patterns that you have outgrown. You know the gifts and compromises of each. Either choice is ultimately okay because you will continue to grow regardless of the outer form of your life. But you do have a choice. And the choice is completely up to you.

"Thank you." Annie's eyes were now like twin suns shining, fully alive and present in this pivotal life moment. She stood at her personal crossroads as she saw the real decision to make. Now her real work would begin and, eventually, would lead her to the right outer decision about her marriage.

## Sadness and Letting Go: Do You Want a Dog?

***In letting go, you may feel grief. The presence of grief does not mean that you've made a bad decision; it shows you care, and have a heart.*** Grief shows that you are sensitive to the feelings of others, and you feel remaining attachment and love for the person or life situation you once embraced, and now are releasing. Allow the sadness as part of your integration, but don't let it cloud your decision about what's right for you. I had a vivid experience of this teaching many years ago.

Kenn and I sat on the Berkshire porch of my friend Kate, a smart psychotherapist I'd been best friends with since we were ashram twenty-two-year-olds. Kenn and I were in tears as we shared our tale of woe. We had recently given our dog Angel away. The adoptive family were caring people who lived in the country and had a little girl named Rebecca. Rebecca had been praying for her parents to allow her to have a dog for two years, her prayers assisted by nuns who were family friends. That our dog was named Angel cracked the nuns up when they learned of Rebecca's victory.

The family had synchronistically come into our life to interview me for a newspaper article about my paintings, Rebecca in tow. Rebecca and Angel bonded instantly when they met. They arrived on the very day Kenn and I had decided we simply were gone too frequently to give Angel the family he deserved and needed. We loved him, but as busy professionals we had to face that we were not the right humans for him. We felt very adult and clear about our decision.

But when we saw Angel drive off smiling in the back seat of this family's car, with an ecstatic Rebecca hugging him, we completely lost it. Kenn ran into the house sobbing, me in hot pursuit. We were stunned to realize how deeply our dog had embedded himself into our hearts. Everywhere we looked, we felt the loss of Angel. Here's where he waits at the door for us to come home, there's where he lies at our feet, oh God—an empty space where his bed used to be, and so on.

We were emotionally totaled. We woke up crying in the night, devastated by our loss. We felt we'd made a terrible mistake. We felt ripped off! We wanted our dog back! We irrationally felt mad at the wonderful, loving family now enjoying our great dog. "Why should *they* have him?" we asked unreasonably. Had it not been for Rebecca's young age and rampant joy, we would have taken Angel back.

Now we sat on Kate's porch desperate for her help. We shared our drama as Kate listened thoughtfully. Then she raised an eyebrow. "I have a question for you," she said. "Do you *want* a dog?"

"No!" we both said in unison.

Kate shrugged and stood up. "Well, we're done. Let's go have some iced tea." We all laughed at her clear question which cut through our teary confusion.

Now, *"Do you want a dog?"* has become a household mantra we use when torturing ourselves over major decisions, a way to get down to the core truth of the matter. We may have attachment, sentiment, sadness as we let go of something, or someone, or some form we once chose, but we may no longer actually be in resonance with that form. Sadness is healing and tears are cleansing, but when sadness arises, feel it and distinguish your truth. Do you really *want* this dog?

*. . . allow breathing space for the new you emerging in your life experience.*

## Can You Inhabit Your Old Forms in New Ways?

*Sometimes, our marriages and jobs, our partners and lifestyles are able to shift and change with us in complementary ways. Sometimes they cannot.* We need not necessarily leave our partners, end our jobs, and move across the country because we have internally grown and changed. However, the way we *inhabit* those old forms must change for us to remain alive and joyful within them, and to keep on track with our soul curriculum.

It's worth taking time with long-held commitments to creatively, thoughtfully see what's possible for change and evolution within that form, to allow breathing space for the new you emerging in your life experience. If you then decide to move forward and release a living situation, job, or relationship in your life, you will do so free of guilt or concern that you didn't try hard enough to make it work or didn't give it enough of a chance.

Trouble arises when a partner or job pulls on us to remain locked into who we used to be, while our Spirit wants to move forward. The trappings of our old lives can begin to chafe and bind. We want to fly and we can't spread our wings. Something has to give. Often what gives is the old form, a shattering or breaking of what is enclosing us.

In making big, life-changing decisions, go slowly at first, being wise and honoring of what you have created in the past, and kind toward others' feelings whose lives are entwined with yours. Introspection, seeking support from a wise counselor or mentor, meditation, asking for guidance, and journaling, all help you clarify what is really going on inside of you and discover how best to meld that—or not—with your current commitments.

When you are integrating an ending in your life, for a time it's good to see if you can honor your old commitments and choices and still shine as the new being you are becoming. Take time to see if your old forms of life can harmonize with the new soul directions calling you.

You may find creative ways to recreate how you are in your job or partnership so that it aligns with the new woman or man you are becoming. If you later find you need to make an external break, you will have the peace and strength of knowing you truly tried to work it out without dramatic outer shifts. You'll then move forward in new directions feeling clear that you are making right choices for yourself.

## Moving On Prematurely

A woman from one of my "Navigating Change" workshops was on the phone for a one-time coaching session. "I have decided to give up my house and my Nia Dance Studio which I founded, and move to St. Croix!" she said excitedly. "I love the Virgin Islands, and can lead Nia at the resorts there. I have a good friend there. I've already bought a house there. I'm all packed for the airport and leave this week. I just wanted to get your support for this move." I sat in the sun breathing deeply and praying for guidance.

I knew she must be feeling insecure about her decision or she would not have asked for the session. She was asking me to support this move that was completely in place, and it's important we honor what someone is ready to do and asking for. Her vision for her new life was actually a wonderful one that aligned to many joys of hers. It might have been just perfect, but I sensed she was burning all her bridges too quickly. The fantasy of perfect happiness in her new life was so great that there wasn't really room for her to consider right timing and personal readiness.

In making decisions to end a form and move on in our lives, we need to not imagine that our problems will all now disappear and life will have a fairy-tale quality. We must be moving from wholeness, not seeking for wholeness outside of ourselves through new outer forms. I trusted that her experience would give her just what her soul needed right now. With her decisions in place and her belongings packed, I wished her well and offered my positive support for her new chapter.

Three months later she called me from her cell phone: "Christine, I'm in New Jersey, driving home from the airport,

*We must be moving from wholeness, not seeking for wholeness outside of ourselves through new outer forms.*

back to my house. Nothing worked out. My St. Croix house had mold and plumbing leaks, and the walls had to be torn down. I moved in with my good friend, but I was so stressed that it strained our friendship, which I'd counted on so much. She broke off our relationship and asked me to leave. The Nia class possibilities at resorts didn't pan out; there were no openings for teachers. I had no friend, no job, and nowhere to go. I decided to go back home, and now I'm driving back."

I felt compassion for her human predicament. I encouraged her to find the positive lessons received and guided her to create a vision for moving back home which would help her focus her energies positively. I wished her well, trusting that she would pull from this experience great lessons which would serve her in moving on.

It is true that we may shine more easily in different jobs, relationships, or physical places. But in deciding to release the old forms of our lives, it's wise to know that the issues in our lives do not vanish with an external move. They just show up in new packages. We must find the sustaining Source within us and do our human healing work in order to be fully ready to move on.

## True Readiness for Big Moves

*Our inner Self knows when change is calling, but we may need time and growth to be fully ready to heed the call.* For years before I had even set foot in New Mexico, I had a recurring intuitive feeling that I would someday live there. The notion of Santa Fe came up for me often as my own promised land, although I had never been out West, save trips to California to teach workshops and visit my sister. I once bought a wooden Star of God mirror for my

New England home, a common architectural feature in Santa Fe, although I did not know that. When I brought it home from the furniture store, I noticed that the tag on the back of the mirror said "Santa Fe Mirror." As I hung the mirror in my Massachusetts house, I intuitively thought, "This will look great in my Santa Fe home," then stopped myself: "What am I thinking?" At the time I was not considering moving west.

I had intuitively sensed the life that was calling me, but I had to wait to be internally fully ready. I had much personal empowerment to gather. It's no good to do something wild and free in your life, then fall apart when you get there. I had not yet fully reclaimed the self-confidence and inner strength to release my home, marriage, and corporate career. I needed to make sure my vision was not just a fantasy, but a true longing of my soul. When I was truly ready, I knew it, and everything unfolded.

To enact a major outer change, you must be ready for some anxious nights on the couch with a box of Kleenex, times of loneliness and so-called failures, and be able to digest life's learning moments without disintegrating. You must have done enough inner healing work that you carry with you a core of clarity and strength.

When you are sure of your readiness, you will move forward on solid ground with yourself. You'll know that while you cannot move away from yourself, you may find a new energy and consciousness supporting your greatest good that will be a blessing to you. Take time, be sure you're right, feel and seek inner guidance. And when you're ready, you will know it with all your heart and move on. Follow your dreams, listen to your call, and see what inner clarity and chops you want to develop so you will be truly prepared internally for a big move.

*Here is a test to find whether your mission on Earth is finished. If you're alive, it isn't.*

≋* RICHARD BACH

## Wherever You Go, There You Are

*When you enact a major shift in your life, remember that you take all of yourself with you.* Teaching a "Navigating Change" workshop, I had just shared my story of moving to Santa Fe many years before to pursue my dream of being a painter. I noticed a young woman sitting in the front row, brow furrowed and lips pressed tightly together as if holding back waves of suffering and sadness. As I finished my tale, she burst out, "I want your life!" giving me pause. "I'm a graphic designer in New York City," she shared, "and I'm miserable. I long to be a fulltime fine artist and live in a beautiful, sunny place like Santa Fe. In fact, I've thought of moving there. Nothing is working for me in New York. I hate my job, but I need the money. I have no time to paint. I want exactly what you have."

How understandably human it is to think that a dramatic outer move will eliminate our inner pain. "Everything that has manifested in my outer life is the direct result of decades of deep inner work," I said gently. "Years of inner work, therapy, and reflection preceded this big move in my life." I wanted to spare her the experience of my erstwhile St. Croix client, while still nurturing her dreams of her new life.

"When you enact a major shift in the outer form of your life, beware of having a fantasy that an external move will resolve unhealed emotional pain and inner problems," I told her. "Wherever we go, there we are. I moved to Santa Fe knowing in advance that I would have times of loneliness and challenges. I knew my own insecurities. I had dug the inner ground of my healing work."

I saw her face fall and rushed to reassure her. "However! If you want to move to Santa Fe and paint, by all means, do so! A new environment may support you in doing the inner work needed right now, which is the true cause of your pain—not New York City or a dead end job. Go with joy. Enjoy creating a new life there for yourself. Just remember this: Move on *consciously*, knowing you will still have to face and heal the same inner dragons. Whatever emotions and issues you have not healed will eventually resurface. They do not disappear in a new place.

"But the light and beauty and atmosphere of Santa Fe, or another place you cherish, may support you in feeling more positive and hopeful in doing your inner work better than your current situation. Follow your heart. Just move on *consciously*." She nodded through her tears. I wished her happiness in whatever she chose.

# Finding True Forgiveness:
# Fully Human, Fully Divine

**F**orgiveness work is a blend of nitty-gritty emotional human healing work and profound spiritual practice. We need to be authentic and integrated in our human healing work before we can attain full forgiveness. In the span of one day, you might inwardly extend full-hearted loving kindness and forgiveness to someone who has hurt you, then later find annoyance, blame, or anger rising toward that same person. This is normal. It demonstrates the need for you to continue unraveling your own emotional ball of yarn—the journey through which you entered into relationships and situations that created pain. When you have integrated your authentic human healing work with deep spiritual practice, your forgiveness eventually becomes complete. You know you are complete in your forgiveness when you no longer obsessively review past circumstances with another with anger or blame. When you take back your power over your own well-being, you feel peaceful, and you are free.

*The truth is, unless you let go, unless you forgive yourself, unless you forgive the situation, unless you realize that the situation is over, you cannot move forward.*

⇒ STEVE MARABOLI

To illustrate the major forgiveness challenge in my own life, I share next my journey of forgiveness with my mother. The step-by-step teachings of practicing forgiveness follow my story.

> ❧
>
> *The dark thought, the shame, the malice,*
> *meet them at the door laughing*
> *and invite them in.*
>
> *Be grateful for whatever comes,*
> *because each has been sent*
> *as a guide from beyond.*
>
> ⇒✴ RUMI, *"The Guest House"**

## From Human to Holy: The Road to True Forgiveness

It was 1986, and I was sitting on an Indian-bedspread-covered futon on the floor in Marianne's therapy office in her New England farmhouse. I was thick in the jungle of feeling and healing my unfaced emotions from a painful childhood. Kneeling at my side, she urged me forward into feeling and releasing decades of denied rage over the emotional and physical abuse I'd experienced from my mother. Marianne's lively, intelligent brown eyes gazed with empathic concern from behind wire rimmed glasses, framed by playful, pixie white hair. In her safe space, up and out came my ancient anger and rage, messily, dramatically, painfully.

As I drove home that night, I felt a new energy and power humming in my heart and singing in my bones. I had exorcised the antique body armoring and vintage emotional pain that I didn't realize I was carrying. A new spirit and newfound inner power surged through me. I rolled down the car windows and sang in the wind, feeling liberated. The larger possibilities for who I could be, and how I could live, flowed through me like an invitation from my soul. Unchained from so much embodied pain, I could now truly begin my life.

*\*The Essential Rumi, trans. by Coleman Barks*

Do we always need to express old rage, grief, or feelings to be able to truly forgive and heal? Definitely not. But if an event or relationship in your life has been profoundly traumatic, and keeps coming up again and again for you in spite of your thoughtful processing and spiritual practice, it's time to turn around and face and feel what's there. Greet your unexpressed emotion as an old friend coming to you with a gift in her hands. If needed, release your emotion in healthy ways.

As a longtime yoga devotee and meditator, I knew the territory of practicing spiritual forgiveness and compassion by heart. Again and again I had taken my deep desire for healing and forgiveness from this extremely challenging relationship to my altar. The peace I would find in my heart vanished with one explosive, attacking phone call from home, reminding me that my thousands of hours of spiritual practice had not liberated me from the pain and rage of a difficult childhood. I had to get down with my anger and pain, feel it and heal it, before I could find the peace of true spiritual forgiveness.

*If you think you're enlightened, go spend a week with your parents.*

≅✷ RAM DASS

As my mother was still alive, I was re-wounded frequently with each contact and my own well-meaning visits home, ending with the old explosive outbursts and belittlements which had hallmarked my growing-up years. I now see how perfect it was that my mother was still alive, for it forced me to keep facing my feelings and finding my power and personal healing in our relationship. I would have missed the healing and love I later found with my mother, the ultimate integration of my life. What a loss that would have been. In the years we had left before her passing, extraordinary miracles happened and we found together "the holiest spot on earth . . . of forgiveness" that A Course in Miracles speaks of. But not yet!

Grief and sadness usually live underneath unexpressed anger. Once I'd released my anger, I grieved, no longer denying the loneliness of my childhood, an absentee—albeit adoring—Father, and a crazy, raging mother. For the first time in my life, I faced and felt what my childhood and teen years had really been like.

My human healing work was intense, but I was signed up for the liberation on the other side of it all. I wanted to be free. My deep spiritual practice alone had not gotten me there. I had to take my still-wounded woman by the hand and help her heal. I trusted the light that was waiting for me on the other side of this journey through old darkness. I sat over and over at the holy altar of the Kleenex box and wept buckets of tears as Marianne sat in front of me, good-motherly hand on my knee, mirroring back the insanity of my mother and empathizing with the true difficulty I had gone through. We unraveled the ball of yarn from rage to the underlying grief.

## Finding Compassion: Seeing Others for Themselves

*When our hearts break open, compassion can enter.* When the bucket of tears was finally empty, a wave of compassion flowed into that empty space, compassion for my mother. Moving beyond my own story by feeling and healing it allowed me to distinguish myself from my mother and see her in her own human dance. I could now turn my attention to my mother's life. I recognized for the first time her own abusive childhood, bereft of loving parenting, hit and demeaned by her father, surviving a passive Victorian mother, moving through two marriages of betrayal and abandonment. I saw her for herself. What a

*I wondered if that was how forgiveness budded; not with the fanfare of epiphany, but with pain gathering its things, packing up, and slipping away unannounced in the middle of the night.*

≋ Khaled Hosseini

revelation to see others separate from what we need and want and project onto them! This true liberation of love and compassion led to more tears, but this time in compassion for my mother's life experience.

Suddenly I saw my Mother with new eyes: just a struggling secretary, raising two daughters without a husband, with little money, and rarely a friend, trying to get along. Suddenly I felt a surge of love and appreciation for this woman God had given me as a parent. I could now remember her countless loving acts, her big heart, her genuine efforts to care for me mixed in with the abuse and attacks, seesawing between her heart of love and her own projected pain. I saw how after every attack she would extend much love, trying to make up for the pain. I saw her endless generosity in giving gifts to me beyond her financial means, trying to show in things the love she could not always express in relationship. I remembered countless acts of support and great love for me which I'd lost touch with. Authentic forgiveness was born.

*In the present moment, you may even heal the past.*

⇒⋆ THICH NAT HAHN

## Who You Are Is the Result of How You Perceive Events

**We are not the results of our life experiences, but of our perceptions of them.** Now a miracle happened. I found again my profoundly deep love for my mother. Even more healing and beautiful for me, I discovered how much she loved me, and always had. Suddenly, I was the grown-up result of a loving mother, not the wounded, fragmented victim of an abusive one. The old stories were still there, but I hadn't been reading the whole book. I'd missed the great love given to me by my mother and focused only on the chapters of pain. I recreated my view of my childhood experience by shifting my perception. A great wholeness rooted itself in my heart.

I still had to set boundaries and say no to negative behaviors, but these became less frequent. Over the years, we began to build a relationship of joyful, caring bonding. Day trips to craft fairs and art museums, to concerts and luncheons were increasingly deep and fun. Our mutual Irish Leo sense of play and shared extroversion made us harmonious, sometimes zany, co-players in the field of life. She loved to laugh and found delight in my out-of-the-box personality, and I in hers. We navigated the irritating or challenging moments with much more grace and much less drama.

*We are all just walking each other home.*

≡☆ RAM DASS

## Our Painful Relationships Become Our Spiritual Teachers

***Everyone desires to love and be loved, but unhealed pain can distort or block that love from showing up.*** After my mother discovered that she had Alzheimer's, she was released from her past and entered the realm of the present moment. Over time, she literally transformed into the person she had always been under all the unhealed pain of the past. Her true nature was freed of past stories, and it stepped forth to shine. It was extraordinary to see what pure light exists when we can let go of our stories about others and our lives.

She forgot about all the past events that had clouded her capacity for happiness and love. She shed all identity related to past losses and entered deeply into what Eckhart Tolle calls "the power of now." When I'd take her out for a drive, Mom began to lose track of where we were. I once asked her, "Mom, do you know where we are?"

"Why, *certainly*," she said, with her usual elegant dignity. "Where?"

"Why, we're *right here*," she said, and we dissolved into giggles.

While I realize this is not the experience of many others who get Alzheimer's, in my mother's case this illness became a kind of blessing, perhaps a soul choice on her part so that she could create healing with her daughters and leave life in a bubble of pure love, as she did.

Transformed by forgetting her past story, her true big Irish heart came forth. Her face softened and her eyes took on a radiance of love. It was a joy to be with her in public, traveling with a white-haired bodhisattva who experienced everyone as family and saw the oneness and goodness in everything. Her patience and kindness toward others touched my heart and easily exceeded my own. My old adversary was now my spiritual teacher!

In her irresistibly loving presence, irritated waiters melted into little boys basking in her huge mother-love. She reached past their thin veneers of surliness to the human beings wanting to feel connected, seen, and loved. She'd constantly reach out and physically touch strangers as we walked down the street, saying with wonder, "Oh! You are so beautiful!" Their guarded shift from wondering what the scam was to realizing the genuineness of her love was a joy to behold and witness. "I love you!" she would declare to them, over and over, touching their arms and smiling, wanting them to know. The love that came back to her everywhere she went was an absolute miracle.

"I love you," she told me and my sister Betsy, over and over, tugging at our sleeves, smiling into our faces. "You are beautiful. I love you so much." Pure healing, pure love! She knew our names to the very end and lit up when we came into the room, no matter how much of her memory had gone. She became our child. Suddenly in a karmic twist of fate, we had all the power and used it to protect and support her, to insure she had the most loving care possible, to love her.

In my last visit with my mother, in her beautiful residence for those with Alzheimer's, I crawled into bed beside her and hugged her as she was napping. Her eyes popped open, "OH!" then softened into a smile, as she realized that she was being held in the arms of her daughter. It had been decades since anyone had lain beside her, holding her lovingly in their arms.

"Mom, I love you so much," I whispered.

"And I love you too, dear."

"All is forgiven, Mom. I have forgiven you, and you have forgiven me."

"Yes, that's right, dear." She drifted off to sleep. The healing release of true forgiveness was ours. She passed on a few weeks later.

*When you meet anyone, remember it is a holy encounter. As you see another, you will see yourself. As you treat another, you will treat yourself.*

≈ A COURSE IN MIRACLES

## The Dance of Forgiveness

**When you stand in the light of your own wholeness, you are able to see beyond others' unconscious or harmful actions.** Forgiveness is essential in navigating change. Without it, we travel forward to our next chapters carrying heavy suitcases of resentment, blame, and hurt. Our lack of forgiveness hurts our own hearts. It puts out the creative fires within us and shrinks our zest for life and positive energies. Our capacity to live in peace and manifest beautiful lives is limited when we do not forgive.

Real forgiveness is not a condescending release of others from their faults, but a gift of inner freedom that we give *to ourselves*. If you are carrying emotional pain from the past you are completing right now, this section is for you. This section gives you a forgiveness map in a step-by-step practice that honors your humanity while remembering your divinity.

True forgiveness ultimately stems from the recognition that you are, and always have been, completely whole and perfect as an individual expression of universal Spirit, or God. And so are all others. *All* others. No one's actions or words can harm or diminish this Divine birthright of your own Being. However, as human beings living our lives here on earth, we need to address our human healing work in healthy ways. Such emotional healing, done authentically, paves the way for you to step into big forgiveness from wholehearted authenticity instead of spiritual loftiness. When your human healing holds hands with your spiritual insight, you feel a rush of freedom from your old stories about the past and other people, a freedom which lightens your path through life.

You are able to recognize the good soul in others, while also seeing clearly and compassionately the blind spots and unfaced shadows behind their harmful actions and words. In this spiritual understanding, balanced with straight, clear human insight, you can release others, stand in your strength, and be free. This is real forgiveness.

*When our feelings come up with a vengeance, so to speak, we have to acknowledge and heal them before we can upshift into authentic forgiveness.*

## A. The Human Side of Forgiveness

### Right Timing and Premature Forgiveness

**When we have suffered in a human relationship, there is a right timing to human healing work and authentic spiritual integration and wholeness.** We need to face our emotional healing work without prematurely transcending it. When our feelings come up with a vengeance, so to speak, we have to acknowledge and heal them before we can upshift into authentic forgiveness. A perfect example of this occurred in one of my "Navigating Change" workshops.

A young woman raised her hand and asked, voice trembling, "Christine, how can I forgive my ex-husband?"

"Why do you need to forgive him?"

"Well, just two weeks after our honeymoon, I found out that he was having sex with my best friend. It ripped my whole life apart. I had to leave him. I now need to forgive him." Her eyes were swimming in tears. Her disempowerment and loss of self-esteem were so apparent that she seemed physically shaky, shoulders collapsed forward and head held down.

"Honey, *forget* about forgiveness right now!" I told her, to the obvious relief of the group. "What you need right now is to be human first and recover your power. You need to feel your outrage that your best friend and new husband deceived you and hurt you so badly. Forgiveness will come later, but it's premature for you right now. You need to focus on things that bring you back in touch with your power and wholeness right now, your beautiful big life waiting to be lived. What brings you joy and strength? What are you passionate about?"

She grinned and I saw a spark of strong energy returning. She then began to speak of her dreams to be a professional photographer, her love of her craft, and her vision of showing her work. She came alive and stood up straighter, self-esteem flooding back in. Later she phoned to say she'd found a local therapist who was helping her deal with her loss, anger, and grief.

One year later I received a beautiful invitation to her photography show and a note sharing how well she was doing. She had honored her human healing work in seeking a good therapist to help her heal her emotional wounds, which in turn had liberated her creativity and energy to manifest her dreams. Eventually she can come to forgiveness of her friend and ex-husband, in her own authentic time.

### The Sacred Territory of Human Emotion: The Way Beyond Is Through

> *Crying only a little bit is no use.*
> *You must cry until your pillow is soaked!*
> *Then you can get up and laugh . . .*
> *And if people say,*
> *"Hey, what's going on up there?"*
> *"Ha ha!" sing back.*
> *"Happiness was hiding in the last tear!*
> *I wept it!"*
>
> ⇒ GALWAY KINNELL, "Crying"

**Emotional healing is a doorway giving you access to your magnificence and light, your joy and wisdom.** If you don't walk through that door, you can't get to the light on the other side. Resist the urge to do a spiritual bypass in order to sidestep the messy, gritty work of being human. The way beyond painful feelings is straight on *through* them, allowing release of whatever is present.

When painful emotions are present, recognize and greet them, so that you can reclaim your wholeness from a full-tilt, authentic, embodied place. Your surfacing emotion may not be anger, but grief, tears, shame, or sadness. Whatever is presenting itself, befriend the emotion as a messenger with a gift in its hands. By allowing healthy expression of your feelings, you get the gift it carries for you in its hands. You can unwrap that gift to find the big new life waiting for you inside of it. If you refuse the messenger entrance, you miss receiving his gift. Without the gift, there is no big new life. You may create new forms that please you, but the unhealed feelings of your life will travel with you like a long shadow you drag behind.

### Steps to Take: Tools for Authentic Forgiveness

### 1. What You Feel Can Be Healed

The first step to true forgiveness is to face and embrace your feelings. Begin right here, where you are, with whatever feelings are present. When the pain, grief, or rage feels overwhelming, seek allies and mentors, friends or counselors in whose presence you feel safe to explore your human feelings on the road to healing them.

How do you know you need emotional clearing? Because your emotions come up again and again, no matter how much spiritual attention you are giving to the practice of forgiveness. In this case, it's time to turn around and embrace the nitty-gritty human work calling for healing. There is a great liberation that comes from expelling these old negative feelings, and then clarifying the false patterns and beliefs that underlie them. You do your human healing work to get the freedom and liberation from this old pain.

*Trust Allah, but tie your camel.*

≋ ISLAMIC SAYING

### 2. Practice Long Distance Compassion

We sometimes think we need a dramatic conversation or emotional closure with someone we are forgiving in order to feel complete, but this might not be possible, and might even hook us further into the very dynamics that caused suffering in the first place. What kind of distance do we then need to have from those we are working on forgiving?

You can practice what I call long-distance compassion. The distance to put between yourself and those who have hurt or betrayed you is the distance at which you can stand in your power and your peace, and still send them authentic blessings. You do not need to see them or communicate with them in order to extend your fullest compassion.

### 3. Send Forgiveness and Honor Your Boundaries

To forgive is different from being naive about where someone is or reengaging with that person in your previous ways. Extending forgiveness and compassion takes place first within your own heart and mind. They are not necessarily about returning to an outward relationship with one who once caused you hurt or harm, although in some cases this may yield positive results, depending on the consciousness of the other.

Compassionate forgiveness is an inside job. Realize that while you have done your human healing work and spiritual work, the other person may not yet have changed *at all*. You need astute wisdom to know when outer reconciliation is healthy and desirable for you, or whether to simply extend long-distance compassion. Your priority is your own peace of mind and wholeness, not necessarily the renewal of a relationship that might not honor your greatest good. Trust Allah, but tie your camel.

*In your ultimate truth, you cannot be diminished or suffer for the actions others, unless you choose to give your power away to them.*

### 4. Don't Suffer for the Limits of Another

Another's limitations are not your work to carry. A powerful mantra to use when another has catalyzed suffering for you is, "I do not suffer for the limits of another." Stand in who you are and be free from carrying other's pain-filled choices.

Realize that, as a part of God, you can never actually lose the essence of who you are. No one's actions, however blind or unconscious, can ever affect your true Spirit. You are untouched at the core of your Being. In your ultimate truth, you cannot be diminished or suffer for the actions of others, unless you choose to give your power away to them.

When you remember who you are, you are standing in your true strength and self-love. That stance is an excellent platform from which to extend understanding and move into authentic, deep forgiveness.

## 5. Create Allies, Mentors, Friends, and Supporters

Feel what's present in you emotionally and give it voice in a healthy, non-harming way that lets this energy of pain be safely released, harming no one including yourself. If you feel the need to do so, find a compassionate, wise friend, mentor, coach, or therapist in whose presence you feel uplifted, respected, and seen to facilitate this release and to support your insightful self-exploration. Don't give your power away by choosing a counselor or therapist in whose presence you do not find hope, unconditional love, and positive, grounded healing work.

Remember that therapists, counselors, or coaches, regardless of degrees and licenses, can only offer to you the level of evolution and wisdom from which they live their own lives. Colleges do not award degrees in loving-kindness, insight, and consciousness. Choose carefully any helping professional you allow the honor of supporting you, being

*I am not what happened to me. I am what I choose to become.*

≈✴ CARL JUNG

led from your heart and intuition. Trust your own experience and be guided by it.

## 6. Be the Cartographer of Your Own Human Journey

Take time to map the false beliefs and concepts that led you into making past choices or allowing relationships into your world that did not serve your highest wellbeing. Look with love and compassion on yourself. As you do so, you take charge of your life and choices and cease feeling the victim of others' interactions or desires with you. You will come to realize that you have made some of your past choices from a false premise that you were not whole, a premise which may have blinded you. With that realization, you now take back the power of decision over your life.

## 7. Recognize That All the People in Your Life Did the Best They Could, Including You

We all make every choice from the levels of consciousness and growth we are living from at each moment. If others in your life could have done better, they would have. If you could have made more enlightened choices in the past, you also would have.

Even intentional hurtful actions from others are unconscious cries for help and attention, statements of brokenness or inner pain projected outwards into hurtful actions. When we can see the negative actions of others as unconscious cries for help, we stand in our own dignity and power to internally extend our compassion and forgiveness.

In this clear state of understanding, we can objectively see that any apparently negative words and actions being sent our way are nothing more than others' misguided

*The holiest spot on earth is where an ancient hatred has become a present love.*

≋ A COURSE IN MIRACLES

attempts to feel good about themselves, however crazily expressed. While removing ourselves from the influence or field of those acting out in hurtful ways, we can also see the wounded parts of others calling for love, recognition, and help. We can remember the liberating truth that we all are doing the best we know how to do, at our current levels of evolution and consciousness, to feel good, to feel whole, and to be loved.

## B. The Spiritual Side of Forgiveness

**In the highest truth, we are one with everyone and interconnected with all who live.** No one can be left out of our hearts because, in the greatest spiritual and quantum reality, everyone is literally connected to us. Everyone in our life experience, past or present, matters. Seen in this light of oneness, forgiveness becomes a profound spiritual act of love, our gift to the world, as well as to ourselves for inner peace. What we embody—bitterness, negativity, and blame, or peace, compassion, and love—is what we extend to the entire world, not only the one we are forgiving. What we focus upon and feel becomes *us*.

### *Practices for Spiritual Forgiveness*

When you have done your human healing work, gathered back your power, seen with spiritual discernment the predicaments and wounds of others, and found compassion born from your insight, you stand in your own wholeness, worth, and well-being. You're at the threshold of spiritual forgiveness. Here are some practices to light your way. Each principle has a guiding quote to inspire your practice.

*If we could read the secret history of our enemies, we should see sorrow and suffering enough to disarm all hostility.*

≋❋ HENRY WADSWORTH
LONGFELLOW

## 1. From Your Place of Power, Look with a Heart of Compassion on Those You Need to Forgive

Compassion is the golden doorway that lets us walk into the liberation of full, authentic forgiveness. Through the depths and honesty of your authentic human healing work, you are now standing on the ground of your own powerful strength and clarity. You have remembered the integral wholeness that is you. From this ground of wholeness, you can now look on others in your past with compassion. You can see with empathy and feeling the dilemmas, struggles, pains, and blindness of your former perceived persecutors and those who have hurt you.

## 2. Be the Big Soul

In any difficult relationship, the more conscious person in the relationship is called upon to be the one to extend understanding and healing. If you're reading this book, this is probably you. To do this, once you have done any needed human healing work, you have to give up living in victim consciousness, seeing yourself at the helpless effect of others' blind choices.

You are now called upon to step up to the spiritual plate of your own larger consciousness and stand in your Higher Self, your own inner light. You are called upon by life to *be* the great soul you actually are, extending forgiveness, understanding, and compassion. Give up waiting around for the other to apologize or show remorse. Don't give your peace and power away to the current consciousness level or limited capabilities of another. Rather than waiting for someone else to give you whatever you mistakenly thought you lacked, claim it for yourself, and then extend it to them in your thoughts and intentions.

*Honor the highest within yourself; for it is the power on which all things depend, and the light by which all life is guided.*

*Dig within. Waste no more time talking about great souls and how they should be. Become one yourself!*

≫ MARCUS AURELIUS

*Have compassion for all beings, rich and poor alike; each have their own suffering.*

✳ THE BUDDHA

Now *you* are the one who inwardly says from your soul to the soul of the other:

> *I remember now who I truly am.*
> *I stand in my strength, love, and wholeness, complete*
>     *in knowing I am an expression of the Infinite*
>     *Spirit, and so are you.*
> *From my place of loving power, I see your own pain,*
>     *your wounds, and your blind spots.*
> *I see your own struggles that caused you to say or do*
>     *things that I experienced as painful.*
> *I bless you. I extend to you my compassion for your*
>     *own suffering and challenges.*

### 3. Recognize the Predicaments of Yourself and Others

The American spiritual teacher Ram Dass describes the circumstances of our human lives as our "predicament." What human predicament is our embodied soul here to work out? What cast of characters have we drawn to ourselves to help us wake up to who we are? How has the presence of a hurtful, disappointing, painful person or situation actually been a golden gift to bring us back home to our own inherent wholeness, our goodness, our beauty, dignity, and power? Can we be the one who is big enough in Spirit to stand and live in our true Selves, and to be the one extending compassion for another's suffering? In our compassion, we are really on the road to forgiveness.

### 4. Conscious Compassionate Detachment: Liberation from Others' Dramas

If compassion is the loving heart of forgiveness, then detachment is its complement. We need both. Compassion

*Patient with friends and enemies, you accord with the way things are.*

*Compassionate toward yourself, you reconcile all beings in the world.*

≈✴ LAO TZU,
*Tao Te Ching*

is rooted in the heart of empathy, kindness, and caring. Detachment is rooted in the wise mind of inner discrimination. It is a clear-minded separation of who you know yourself to be from the dramas and predicaments of another.

When you sit in wise detachment, you realize that you have nothing at all to do with the crazy, hurtful, disappointing actions of others. You see with crystalline clarity that there is another human being over there trying to do the best he can, functioning from his own unhealed wounds, needs, and blindness, and thus acting out of those wounds to cause pain. You have compassion for his predicament, but you also see him with detachment.

Detachment brings objectivity about another's predicament. Objectivity brings clarity and liberation. You are now free from suffering the effects of another's dance of ego and fear. You see it all with a mixture of clear love, compassion, and clarity. You may say to yourself:

*Lord, make me an instrument of Your peace.*

≋❋ St. Francis

> *I see the deeper truth of this situation now. These actions of others that evoked my own unhealed places are just a reflection of their own pain, wounds, and hurts. I did not cause them, and I am not responsible for them. They will find their own ways to heal as I find my own path.*
>
> *I am free, and they are free.*

## 5. Lech Lecha—Living as a Blessing to the World

Big Sur, California, is one of my soul places on earth. Although I've been visiting there for thirty years, every time I return to Big Sur, I am opened up in some special way, as if my soul evolves and positively expands there in a new way with each trip. I don't feel called to move there,

*Sentient beings are numberless. I vow to save them all.*

❋ Buddhist Vow

but choose to hold it as a soulful, inspiring place of refuge and retreat in my life.

On one trip there in the beauty of winter on the California coast, I was waiting for the scrumptious breakfast provided at the historic Big Sur Inn. I stood by a Toyota with a bumper sticker that said *"Lech Lecha."* Two women strolled over, a couple enjoying a respite from their L.A. life. I asked one of them, "What does *lech lecha* mean?" She corrected my fractured Hebrew pronunciation with a little grin and I repeated it with my best *shikseh* Jewish accent. Then she said, "It's from the Old Testament. It means: Go forth and be a blessing to the world." I loved that these two women drive around proclaiming our inborn ability to be a blessing to everyone, everywhere we go. Part of that blessing is the extension of our forgiveness to everyone we are able to, even if that forgiveness takes time and works in incremental ways.

As a practice of forgiveness, extend your *lech lecha*—being a blessing—in little situations: irate drivers who blow their horns at you, crabby people who vent their annoyance irrationally in public. Even when you feel like returning negativity, which is only human, you can be aware of the outcome you want and choose to extend blessing silently. Extending forgiveness and blessing takes place in your mind. You don't need to speak or even smile at anyone; just quietly, in your mind, say, "Bless you," or "I forgive you," which means, "I see the good soul in you and let go of all the rest."

## 6. The Real Work: Blessing Those Who Intend Harm

A story about the Dalai Lama demonstrates extending blessing in the presence of overt attack. The Dalai Lama was in Japan, and as he strolled through a crowd, a young woman began angrily screaming at him. He lifted his hand in the universal gesture of blessing and harmlessness and blessed her across the crowd of people, over and over. This story touched me deeply. He could hear her pain and inner strife in the crazy acting out of rage toward him, and chose to extend his forgiveness and blessing. In that moment, a small piece of the pain in the world was healed in his gesture.

We can choose to extend blessing even though we may feel angry in the moment and not be as elevated yet as the Dalai Lama. One day I parked my car at one of my favorite Santa Fe coffee bars. When I got out, a woman standing by the car next to me began screaming at me that I had parked badly and her husband couldn't get out of his huge SUV, which straddled more space than his parking spot provided. I felt my Irish temper flare up inwardly and my ego inclination to tell her off grandly arise. Instead, I pointed out tensely that I was squarely between the parking space lines. She then began to insult the kind of car I was driving! She needed someone, or something, to vent her anger at, even if it was my trusty old Toyota.

My ego wanted to retaliate, but I gritted my teeth, put coins in the meter, and walked away, scolding my ego, "Don't say anything! You are angry, but just bless this woman. Bless her and forgive this crazy behavior." I said to her in my mind, "Bless you. Bless you. I forgive you." I did this not because I am a saint—far from it—but in spite of my anger. I wanted to feel peace of mind on this beautiful day, not negativity, and I knew I had a choice and control over that outcome.

As I calmed down and bought my latte, I reflected how much inner pain this woman must be in to attack total strangers—and their cars!—in public. I felt compassion for her predicament. I remembered that she is a part of me in the biggest truth of life and our interconnection

*Be the change you wish to see in the world.*

⇒ MAHATMA GANDHI

*Hatred never ceases by hatred*
*But by love alone is healed.*
*This is the ancient and eternal law.*

*Like a caring mother*
*Holding and guarding the life*
*Of her only child,*
*So with a boundless heart*
*Hold yourself and all beings.*

*May I and all beings be filled with*
*loving kindness.*
*May I and all beings be safe from inner*
*and outer dangers.*
*May I and all beings be well in body*
*and mind.*
*May I and all beings be happy and free.*

❁ THE BUDDHA

with one another. I sent to her what I hope someone would send to me in a moment of total insanity: blessings and forgiveness.

## 7. Be the Change

When you authentically forgive someone in your past or present, with your humanness and your divinity holding hands, you become a blessing to the entire world. You become part of the light-force of those giving to the world, not those seeking to fill imaginary holes in their inner buckets. You move through your life giving your compassion and blessings to others as often as you can. Your ability to be a blessing to the world is grounded in your deep human healing work, your clarity and insight about the dynamics driving negative behaviors of you and others in your life, and your sense of the bigger picture of your interconnection with all others. When this happens, you are living in your peace, power, and wholeness. You have forgiven the past. You are a blessing to the world.

# Ending with Grace, Gratitude, and Completion

*In your endings are the seeds of your beginnings.* As you end situations, jobs, and relationships in your life, the trail you leave behind you is your legacy. It shapes what's to come in your life by setting the energetic stage for your new beginnings.

The manner in which we end something sets the template for what we create next. When we leave a form in our lives that has been part of us, we need to be aware of what we are leaving behind us. We cannot cut free of relationships, jobs, places, and friendships in a messy way that leaves bad feelings, dishonored debts, muddy relationships, or negativity, and then hope to create a shiny new life of joy and goodness. Looking backward on our endings, we want to see a clean wake behind us. We do what's in our power to end well.

## Leaving a Clean Wake Behind You

For fourteen years, Kenn and I spent summers living on Lake Mahkinac in Stockbridge, Massachusetts, while I taught

*The manner in which we end something sets the template for what we create next.*

programs at Kripalu Center and he ran his art gallery. We had an old, beloved, blue-and-white Sea Ray motorboat, the turquoise Bimini top held together with duct tape and old sarongs, a floating gypsy, bohemian nest. On days off, our boat was our second home; a respite from the world, and a haven in the middle of the lake from which to feed seagulls, read, and nap in the rocking boat between swims. As we boated back to our cabin, I liked to look backward at the wake we left behind us. I wanted to make sure nothing was left in the water by our stay and nothing flew out of the boat, no garbage or personal items left in the frothy water curving out in a white V behind us.

In my corporate trainer years, I was once having dinner in Boston with a client, Seamus. In the 1980s, Seamus ran an award-winning graphic design company. At the time of our lunch, several of his key partners were moving on to other design agencies, as often happens. We were discussing the manner in which each of them had left. Some had gone quickly, taking key clients as they departed, leaving bad feelings after years of teamwork and co-creating. Others had gone as friends, with respect to their old firm, making sure all ends were tied up and positive energy surrounded their departures.

My first husband and partner Paul and I had recently divorced, and were still friends, even doing some corporate gigs together in the beginning. Seamus took a sip of his beer and gazed at me. "You know Christine," he said, "you can tell a lot about a person from the way they end things. I'm looking at my partners. Some don't give a damn about us, some really care, some are taking away clients as they leave, and some have integrity. I'm also looking at you and Paul; how you don't talk negatively about each other, you treat each other with respect, you even still collaborate.

Everything is right there about a person in how they end things."

I didn't end things well as a younger woman. I split abruptly from intentional communities I was part of and carelessly walked away from friendships I'd valued when something new called me forward on my life trail. I am grateful for friends who confronted me about this pattern and stayed in touch with me in spite of myself. They taught me that my leaving does matter, and that I need to do it well.

My personal reason for not ending well was rooted in a deep sense of low self-esteem and a feeling that my presence didn't matter much to anyone. I was operating from old beliefs left over from my childhood, when I had to move nearly every year, and no one seemed to notice that I was leaving. This low esteem, rather than a lack of caring, caused me to appear cavalier in suddenly moving on without saying goodbye, or acknowledging who and what I was leaving.

As I healed my human story over the years, I have changed the way I end things. I pay attention to the trail I'm leaving behind me. I do my best to honor old forms and friendships coming to completion in my life, and end as consciously and positively as possible. I know that how I end fuels how I move forward to the next form in my life.

## Gratitude for the Good

*When you are ending something in your life, the practice of gratitude for what you are leaving puts you in a positive energetic space of acknowledging the good that was present and blessed you.* When my first husband Paul and

*Do what you must with another human being, but never put them out of your heart.*

≋⋆ KABIR

I ended our ten-year marriage, I discovered the power of gratitude to make our ending positive and more of a blessing for both of us.

The quote shown here by the mystic poet Kabir is one of Paul's favorites, and it describes our divorce process. We had already navigated some hard parts and challenges together. That work was behind us, and in that clarity, we realized our lives were moving on in different directions. It was not an easy decision, but it was the right one for us, arrived at after considerable thought.

For our divorce day, I wrote Paul a gratitude letter thanking him for the good we'd shared. I gave him my letter that morning, before going to court, along with a woven throw for the home we'd shared that would now be solely his. I wanted to make that day a holy day, a positive turning point for us that appreciated who we'd been and what we'd shared. I wouldn't give my power away to the court system or anyone else to dictate how I ended this important part of my life.

Although Massachusetts law requires divorcing couples to stand in court and declare their "irreconcilable differences" to everyone present, I added to the courtroom that Paul and I had great love and respect for each other, and intended to continue as friends. The old Italian judge loved this, and said, "This is wonderful. I wish I saw this more often in my courtroom! Are you two sure you want to divorce?"

"YES," we said in unison. Then we went out to lunch. More than twenty years later, we remain good friends, giving each other good advice when asked, checking in on our big life events, supporting each other's work and cutting up on the phone.

Well, this is all very nice, you may be thinking, but what if you are leaving a relationship in which the other is hostile or blaming, and lacks the consciousness to end well with you? Your feeling of completion is within your power, and is not dependent on what someone else chooses to do or not do. Regardless of another's choices, your peace and well-being are in your own hands.

People sometimes fear noticing the good in a place, person, or situation they are ending with out of a concern that they'll collapse in their resolve to move on. This is false thinking. Let yourself feel the good parts of what is ending so that you acknowledge it all: the challenges, the lessons learned, *and* the good. You'll then move forward enriched by the good that was there. Your gratitude practice gives you emotional freedom and mental clarity as to the rightness of your choice to let go and move forward.

Claim your power to appreciate the good, to take away the lessons you have learned, and be the conscious soul who takes the high road, leaving a clean wake behind you. Your stance in ending and your own good intentions will give you peace of mind and a sense of well-being.

You may say goodbye in your heart and Spirit in many creative ways that give you the feeling of wholeness and completion. When my father died, I had a powerful experience of saying goodbye to him in a most unusual way—through ritual.

*Your feeling of completion is within your power, and is not dependent on what someone else chooses to do or not do.*

## Creating Rituals for Saying Goodbye

**In times of change and transition, rituals give us ways to say goodbye, to integrate and honor what has been, as well as what is being born.** In our Western culture, we've lost much of our ancestors' ancient rituals marking our big life passages. However, you can create your own meaningful rituals to bring closure in your endings with peace and wholeness, contributing to your own full sense of well-being.

My father, Hugh Harris Warren, was my kindred soul and the light of my early years. Although I spent two weeks with him in the hospital close to his death, I missed his funeral. I was an ashram renunciate, living far away, without any funds for the plane ticket. I correctly considered it more important to have been with him while he was still alive. However, I felt a terrible loss in my heart, and felt that I had let his Spirit down by not being there for his service. I needed healing and completion.

My father was a captain in the Merchant Marines, a mythic Welsh-American soul who spent nearly his entire life at sea. He abhorred organized religion as the opiate of the people and the cause of all wars. "We Zoroastrians have no problems with others," he used to joke with me. I discovered later that Zoroastrians are members of a religion originating in ancient Persia.

He loved poetry and the ancient myths, and used to read me to sleep as a child from Edith Hamilton's Greek and Roman mythology. He showed me how to find my latitude and longitude by the stars using his brass sextant, which now sits here in my writing studio. He knew the constellations and taught them to me on his infrequent visits home from the ship. Dad's ashes had been spread at sea in the Gulf of Mexico following the funeral I missed.

It was now twenty years after his passing, and I was taking a workshop at Esalen Institute with the great mythologist Michael Meade. Michael invited anyone on the campus who wished to spend an afternoon down at the ocean creating a group ritual. He didn't define what we'd do or how we'd do it; our group of about fifteen people made it up together.

We hiked down the cliffs and gathered driftwood on the beach, a rugged stretch of the Pacific with crashing surf surging around the huge boulders. We made a human chain, passing driftwood up to the top of a high flat rock, where one man created a large, unlit bonfire. There was silence and focus and energy in our movements together. I had no concept of what this ritual would mean to me, but my soul was very clear about what I needed. As I stood knee-high in the cold Pacific waters, passing timber up, suddenly I saw the bonfire as a funeral pyre for my father.

We finished our huge firewood pile and went in to dinner. Afterward in the starlit night, Michael invited the entire Esalen community to gather in the dark at the cedar fence line edging the cliffs. Down below, the man who had built the bonfire lit the wood, and a huge fire blazed up into the night sky. I stood at the fence and wept.

I gave my father the funeral sendoff he would have loved. I spoke to him about his life and his worth and his immense goodness to me. I told him how he showed me that I am loved and worthy. I wailed my heart out alone at the fence in the night. Mounds of sparks flew out from the huge fire far below us, fanning out over the ocean with bits of red-orange light. I visualized in the sparks a great old sailing ship going out to sea lit on fire, just as the Vikings buried their sea captains in blazing ships. I sent my father all the prayers and love and holy wishes in my bursting heart.

And then, I felt complete. I had said goodbye to my father at last, and done so in this beautiful, potent act of ritual. We were joined in Spirit. He'd gone out to sea in the old ways, in a blaze of light, as he'd have so loved.

"I'm so sorry I wasn't there, Dad," I whispered to my Father's soul.

*God knows the past, present, and future. He will determine the future for you and accomplish the work.*

*What is to be done will be done at the proper time.*

*Don't worry.*

*Abide in the heart and surrender your acts to the Divine.*

≈❋ RAMANA MAHARSHI

"That's OK, sugar," he said back, using his favorite name for me. We were one. I was done. The power of ritual to create moments of healing and completion had healed me.

You create your own rituals according to your intuition. There is no script or plan, just the one you make up for yourself that feels right in your heart. You might light a candle and write a letter to one you are completing with, then take it outside to read and release. You might find an object symbolizing that part of your life you are ending, and float it downstream to the world, place it in a special place in nature, or burn it as an act of release.

## Trusting Divine Plan

There is a Divine plan unfolding right now for your life. There is a guiding wisdom embracing you at the crossroads of your personal change process. On the highest level, your soul has already chosen the next steps for you, the ones that will help you expand and grow in the best way possible.

To hear the guidance of Divine plan in your life, take time daily to meditate and be still. In stillness, you enter the living moment of your life and give up struggling to figure everything out. In the emptiness of meditation and quiet prayer, you can hear the still small voice of God, instead of the anxious, controlling voice of the fearful ego. Solutions, direction, and clarity unavailable through the analytic mind can come through with startling insight and wisdom when you let go of too much mental planning and effort. Every day, take time to meditate, ask for guidance, and listen.

You are where you should be. You will know what to do, where to go, and how to follow your own right timing if you take time daily to be still and listen to the inner wisdom of your soul. Your peace and well-being are already established by God. Get out of your own way and let that peace and Divine guidance show you the way to go. In your inner stillness, you will know what direction to take, what decision blesses and expands your growing Self. You will know when you are honestly prepared to move on. And when you do enact a big outer shift, it will be from the wholeness inside of you, not looking outside of yourself for it. Your new change will then be a blessing to you, and you will move on in wholeness.

*You have ended well. You are now ready to move on in your journey of Navigating Change. You stand at the crossroads of your life between your old path and the new one you are about to embark on. It's time to feel the ground of this intersection right here and now, in the present moment.*

*Turn the page to enter Phase 2: The Mystery: Time To Retreat And Reflect.*

# PHASE 2

# THE
# MYSTERY

*Time to Retreat
and Reflect*

# PHASE 2

✣

# The Mystery:
# Time to Retreat and Reflect

The transformational cycle of a caterpillar into a butterfly is one of nature's great mysteries. When the caterpillar has gathered the food it needs to create a new form, it attaches to a branch and spins a cocoon around itself, a kind of nest in which it can retreat from its former caterpillar life and prepare for the transformation to come. Within the cocoon, the caterpillar actually dissolves, turning into a gelatinous fluid. Within that fluid are what entomologists call "imaginal cells," which in time give birth to a butterfly. The beautiful being that eventually emerges is the direct outcome of this time of retreat, imagining, and rest. The dissolution of the caterpillar creates one of the most beautiful life forms on the planet, the butterfly.

The Mystery Phase is the time between forms in your life. The old you has died, but the new one has not yet been born. You are hanging in the air between trapeze bars, wondering if the next bar will show up to swing on. You are like the caterpillar, preparing to change form, but first needing a safe cocoon in which to curl up, dissolve, and shapeshift. Time and space are needed for this extraordinary process.

*What the caterpillar calls the end of the world, the Master calls a butterfly.*

≋ LAO TZU

It's time to allow space for what is being born in you to grow, then emerge at the perfect time.

Going through the Mystery can feel chaotic and confusing. Your old identity is dissolving, but the new one is not yet full-blown. You are in the Mystery, the space in life where you've released the old, but cannot yet see the new. This section provides travelling instructions to support you in your time in the Mystery, your life's metamorphosis.

## Phase 2: The Mystery guides you through:

# Time in the Cocoon

## Obeying the Natural Rhythms of Life

**W**hen we're in the Mystery Phase, we must be aware not to rush new forms into life before they are **ready.** In Nikos Kazantzakis' great novel *Zorba the Greek*, Zorba learned the importance of trusting the unfoldment of the eternal rhythms of life, the Divine plan.

*We should not hurry, we should not be impatient, but we should confidently obey the eternal rhythm.*

⇛✲ Nikos
Kazantzakis,
*Zorba the Greek*

*"I remember one morning when I discovered a cocoon in the back of a tree, just as a butterfly was making a hole in its case and preparing to come out. I waited a while, but it was too long appearing and I was impatient. I bent over it and breathed on it to warm it. I warmed it as quickly as I could and the miracle began to happen before my eyes, faster than life. The case opened; the butterfly started slowly crawling out, and I shall never forget my horror when I saw how its wings were folded back and crumpled. The wretched butterfly tried with its whole trembling body to unfold them. Bending over it, I tried to help it with my breath, in vain.*

*"It needed to be hatched out patiently, and the unfolding of the wings should have been a gradual process in the sun. Now it was too late. My breath had forced the butterfly to appear all crumpled, before its time. It struggled desperately and, a few seconds later, died in the palm of my hand.*

*"That little body is, I do believe, the greatest weight I have on my conscience. For I realize today that it is a sin to violate the great laws of nature. We should not hurry, we should not be impatient, but we should confidently obey the eternal rhythm.*

*"I sat on a rock to absorb this New Year's thought. Ah, if only that little butterfly could always flutter before me to show me the way."*

What butterfly is in your soul-life, preparing to emerge at the right time from the protective cocoon? Could your butterfly be a physical relocation, a new home? A new professional direction? A loved one coming in to share your life? A creative urge getting ready to shake itself off and express itself through you? Are you blowing on the cocoon, trying to rush the butterfly out so you can enjoy its beauty?

Consider well the new life growing inside you right now, and allow your magnificence time to gestate. Have faith that by waiting and trusting the Divine mystery, the butterfly of your new Being will emerge at the right time, fully formed, able to spread its wings and fly on. *Be* in the Mystery, rest for a time in the cocoon, and know that what is happening inside of this time in your life is going to create your new Self to come.

*In the depth of winter, I finally learned that within me there lay an invincible summer.*

≋ Albert Camus

## Time in the Mystery to Rest and Heal

**At the thousand-year-old Taos Pueblo in New Mexico, the Indians close the pueblo to visitors for the month of January.** They only wear moccasins or soft-soled shoes on the earth for that time. They believe the earth—a living Mother—is sleeping, and should not be disturbed by heavy footsteps, tourists bearing cameras, cars, activity, or superfluous movement. Their own back yard is the pueblo land of their ancestors. They walk softly on the earthen ground of their ancestral plaza in winter's deep time, while the earth rests in her own Mystery. Intimately involved with their own land, desert, and mountains, the elders who remember the old ways mirror this quiet time in their lives. There is nothing in this passage to plant, grow, or harvest; all activity is behind for this season. It is time to rest and dream by the fire, eat what has been gathered, and be still in the Mystery of all things.

In Phase 2 of change, like the Pueblo Indians in winter, we cocoon for a time, allowing ourselves to rest in the Mystery of not knowing what's next. We gaze back on our lives with all of our doing, activity, planning—all passed and fallen now. Gone. As old forms have passed away, we need to take time to take stock; take time as our lives allow to sit back and reflect. In fear of the void and of releasing their outward personae for a time, foolish ones rush forward into the next big form, so they can say "I live here, I work there, this is my lover, and I am a . . . ."

Wise ones know to rest for a time in simply knowing: I am. I am here, now. I trust that embracing my own passage through the Mystery is going to lead me forward in my life at the perfect time, in the perfect way, to the

*Wise ones know to rest for a time in simply knowing: I am. I am here, now.*

*I'll learn to love the
    fallow way
When winter draws the
    valley down
The crystal time, the
    silent time
I'll learn to love their
    quietness
While deep beneath the
    glistening snow
The black earth dreams
    of violets
I'll learn to love the
    fallow way.*

≈ JUDY COLLINS,
    "The Fallow Way"

perfect people, places, and situations that bless me most. For now, I am retreating and doing nothing external, and that is fine and beautiful. My retreat has a solemn dignity and goodness in it. I am living in the Mystery of my life for this time period. All is well. There is nothing to do but be here now, and let my life unfold.

## How Did That Turn Into This? Teachings from the Seasons

**When we're in the Mystery, we take time to find answers to life's important questions.** Sweeping away mounds of golden leaves on my Santa Fe garden deck for morning yoga one November, I recalled doing yoga in the same spot in early spring, with small green buds just opening. I remembered full-blown waves of green leaves sweeping the deck, lifting and falling in summer's breezes. Then came the blaze of foliage, burning gold and scarlet, and apples on the ground, chewed with the nocturnal gnawings of resident bears and coyotes. And now, these same leaves lay faded and scattered on the deck beneath bare branches. It seemed impossible that all of these changes had flown by in the months between March and November. I asked myself, "How did *that* turn into *this?*"

We ask ourselves how who we once were turned into this woman, this man we are *now*. What was the process we went through to arrive at this point? What catalyzing events and experiences made us stop and question how we were living, loving, and working? Who did we let into the door to our hearts? What moments were awakenings, making us realize we need to move on and let go? What soul-parts of us were knocking on the door, asking for change?

Such reflection requires time out, space in your life in which you are not trying to move your life forward for a while. Even if you must attend to work that brings in needed income, even if you are caring for children and family, you need to creatively carve out time for personal reflection and retreating, time for not-doing, in order to ask yourself these questions. You may take off weekends, go into nature, go away to a quiet retreat, or find early morning and evening time to be still and write, feel your heart, and reflect on these important life-change questions.

Only in the silence and quiet of retreating and reflecting can you hear your own inner voice, answering your questing from a place beyond thinking and drawing on what you *used* to know. And when you hear the answers to your questions, write them down, or draw them, keep them with you, and let their wisdom be the imaginal cells in your change journey, one day turning you into something wildly beautiful, born from all you once were.

*Only in the silence and quiet of retreating and reflecting can you hear your own inner voice . . . .*

# The Power of the Present: The Value of Not Rushing Forward

## Making Things Happen: Trying to Move On Prematurely

*Should we make things change in our lives? Or just surrender to Divine plan and let things unfold naturally?* I had this question in my heart while on retreat at Esalen with the Benedictine monk, Brother David Steindl-Rast. I was then in my forties and contemplating getting out of the corporate world and initiating my life as a writer and artist, a radical move I knew would impact my first marriage as well. I couldn't figure out whether to wait and allow things to unfold naturally, or push forward and make things happen. I asked if I might walk him to dinner following an afternoon session. We strolled along the path overlooking the Pacific, as the sun rested on the magenta edge of a watery horizon.

I described my dilemma to Brother David. The rosy peach sunset light bounced off the Pacific waters into his kind eyes. I asked him, "Should we make things change in our lives? Or just surrender to God's will and let them unfold naturally?"

"Ah, a good question, one I have grappled with myself," he reflected, a gentle smile wrinkling his face. "The thing is that we certainly can, with our will, make things happen that could seem very good indeed. But then," he raised his eyebrows and gazed warmly at me, "we may block something much better that God is trying to give us."

Several years passed before I was truly ready to move on from the corporate world and my first marriage; a marriage that was right for me at the time I had entered into it, but which both I and my first husband had outgrown. By waiting, growing, deepening my own consciousness and healing, when I finally felt led to take outer action, the timing was just right. I felt complete, grateful, and deepened by these life experiences. I felt ready to enact my new expression of self in the world. Everything then just unfolded naturally, without effort or pushing.

*Rushing into action, you fail.*
*Trying to grasp things, you lose them.*
*Forcing a project to completion,*
*You ruin what was almost ripe.*

*Therefore the Master takes action*
*By letting things take their course.*
*He remains as calm*
*At the end as at the beginning.*

≈ LAO TZU, *Tao Te Ching*

## Suzanne, the Snake, and the Towers: The Inverse Wisdom of Not Moving On

***Sometimes what we need in order to move forward is to fully embrace exactly where we are.*** Suzanne called me for counseling "to help me move on," as she stated on the

*It may be that when we*
*no longer know what*
*to do*
*we have come to our*
*real work,*
*and that when we no*
*longer know which*
*way to go*
*we have come to our*
*real journey.*

≫* WENDELL BERRY,
*"The Real Work"*

phone. I opened my door to find a lovely woman in her early forties, elegantly dressed, buff from devoted yoga practice, long blonde hair perfectly arranged. In her delicate smile, though, I saw fear and sadness. She arranged herself carefully on my couch, tucking her feet beneath her and crossing her arms over her heart, and began, "I need to move forward in my life, and I'm here to find out how to." In this opening declaration I heard, between the lines, "I am afraid to be right here with my life as it is, right now. I don't know how to be with my feelings, and I'm in a hurry to get away from my past." Suddenly she burst into uncontrolled, shoulder-shaking sobs, while struggling not to cry: "I didn't want to do this! I want to move on!" Ah, the soul-task before us was now clear. And it was assuredly the opposite of "moving on."

Suzanne's story encompassed her personal trauma from one of the greatest tragedies America has faced. Suzanne was married to a kind man who could not express himself emotionally, but was a good provider and a secure comfort to her. She wanted more feeling and energy in her marriage, and had moved out twice, then moved back in, being lonely and missing his supportive presence. He met her moving in and out with equanimity: "Whatever you want is fine." Hardly a response to make her feel passionately wanted and loved!

While struggling to decide what to do about this, she took a walk in Central Park one day, and a snake wriggled across her path. She stopped dead and waited to see what the snake would do. It paused in the middle of the path, sat there for a bit, and then turned around and went back the way it had come. We laughed about how life presents crystal clear symbols of our inner states when we pay attention to them. The snake—symbol of transformation, of death and rebirth—could not decide which way to go, and back-tracked. Like Suzanne.

While in this period of indecision, she went to her job as a corporate manager in Manhattan one day. As she stood in her corner office, looking out the large plate-glass windows facing tall skyscrapers, she watched in horror as a commercial airplane smashed into one of the tall buildings. It was September 11, 2001, and Suzanne was staring at the World Trade Towers. Several of her staff members rushed into her office: "A plane has smashed into one of the towers!" As staff gathered and watched the flames and smoke pouring from the building, minutes passed, and then a second plane smashed into the second tower. Frozen in shock and fear, Suzanne described watching as people leapt to their deaths from the windows of a building much like hers, rather than be immolated inside.

The next day, with the world reeling in grief and shock, she dutifully came to work. Her boss gathered the staff into his large office. Looking at them he announced: "Business as usual." Period, end of story. No room to grieve, to share, to sort out feelings and share support in a time of abject terror and pain. She had to leave the company, so overwhelmed was she with the whole traumatizing experience. Now she was unemployed and living alone, doing hours of yoga and meditation each day, desperately trying to find a way out of her pain and a path to move forward in her life.

We often unconsciously draw into our lives cowork-ers, bosses, lovers, or friends whose behaviors surface old wounds and beliefs needing healing in us. If we use these sand-in-the-oyster relationships well, our protago-nists give us perfect opportunities to confront and posi-tively change our internal limiting beliefs and make good

*. . . our protagonists give us perfect opportunities to confront and positively change our internal limiting beliefs . . . .*

positive progress in our growth. As it turned out, her boss's repressive attitude toward pain mirrored her own family's modus operandi during her formative years. In her childhood, her parents' attitude for dealing with pain and loss was, "Be tough. Get over it. Move on." There was no acknowledgement for pain, despair, grief, or emotion. Everyone had to simply get over the traumas and pains of life somehow and "move on." And following her 9/11 experience, this was predictably the advice from her family: "Get over it. Move on."

Now I sat across from this accomplished, bright woman struggling with a stable but emotionally unfulfilling marriage and a lack of career, who was wondering what was wrong with her for not being able to "get over it." Suzanne needed exactly the opposite of her stated prescription for our work together: she needed to become fully present with herself, *not* move forward, but slow down and feel her feelings. Then she could see where her feelings might lead her.

*It is I who must begin, here and now, right where I am, not excusing myself by saying things would be easier elsewhere . . . to live in harmony with the voice of Being.*

≋✷ VACLAV HAVEL

## Getting a Ph.D. in Transformation

Suzanne made a conscious choice to let go of creating new forms in her life for a while and embrace the inner work at hand. She let go of seeking employment for a time in order to consciously give herself time for her inner journey through the Mystery. She was relieved to let go, but concerned that people kept asking her, "What do you *do?*" To respond to those inquiring about her life work, I told her, "Tell them you're getting your Ph.D. in personal transformation." She loved having a spiritual calling card that described the profound inner work she was engaged in.

Now Suzanne had a program and purpose, one completely inwardly focused. She threw herself into her inner journey, spending time daily in yoga and meditation practice and attending spiritual and personal growth workshops. Our sessions and her retreats and workshops with many teachers gave her needed space to mine the jewels from her life change. Finally letting herself feel and heal a lifetime of denied emotions, Suzanne began to find glimmers of inspiration and a fresh sense of what *she* might like for her life, instead of what others expected of her. Instead of continuing as a corporate manager, she began to weave a vision of opening a yoga center, wedding her love of yoga and spirituality with her considerable business abilities.

By honoring her time in the Mystery, feeling her feelings, allowing grief and uncertainty, and integrating unfaced pieces of her past, she knew intuitively when she was ready to truly move forward into her vision and rich new self-expression in the world. Not moving on for a time had facilitated her true path of moving on, integrated and whole, with new life purpose clearly in place and old denied grief transformed into joy.

## Sonya's Mystery Phase: Letting Go, Turning Inward

Sonya first called me two weeks after her husband's death, after seeing my ad in the Santa Fe paper for a Navigating Change group. I heard her daughter singing in the car as she called me from her cell phone. "My husband was a well-known figure in Santa Fe—high profile," she said. "I haven't cried since he died or really grieved yet." I wondered what feelings needed to bubble to the surface and have a voice

*It is not easy to acknowledge unfinished business with a loved one who has died.*

in Sonya. "I thought your group could help me move on," she said.

Gently I told her I thought the group was premature for her, and her grief work needed to happen first. She was already in therapy with a grief counselor. I invited her to call me in the future. Ten months later, Sonya called about another Navigating Change group. This time her voice had passion and energy in it. I could feel her readiness now to do the group, and accepted her into the group, as well as taking her as a client.

It is not easy to acknowledge unfinished business with a loved one who has died. For all of his positive qualities, her husband Thomas—a charismatic, charming, and well-known figure in Santa Fe—had unwittingly, through the sheer force of his big persona, been a suppressive force for Sonya's still-unformed power and voice. She had married him when insecure and younger, feeling he would give her status and security through his big personality. "I felt I would be *somebody* next to him," she shared. As she matured, however, she realized that she was the one with greater depth, and that he lacked the personal depth and spiritual consciousness she herself possessed. The TV ran all day, despite her protests, and he did not meet her with the deep presence she longed for in a mate.

Significantly, she complained in session that while he was living, Thomas never made deep eye contact with her, something very important to her. She had not felt seen as a child, and repeated this pattern with Thomas. While a huge loss and adjustment for her, Thomas' death was also a liberation for her to claim her own life. At forty-five, she was a woman relishing the freedom of finding her true Self and voice.

A bohemian, artistic woman, with vintage clothes and cowgirl boots, wearing hand-woven blouses from her international art-buying travels, Sonya was extremely present, always sitting across from me with unblinking, deep brown eyes. Her eye contact was so extraordinary I found it hard to envision her living with a partner who did not look into her eyes. She had never been fully seen or acknowledged by anyone, and just needed support in standing in her own inner light.

Put in the shadow by her famous parents, world-class authors who shamed her own writing and expression—literally, undermined her voice—she had replicated her brilliant, charismatic, and unacknowledging father in her marriage to Thomas, beside whom, as with her father, she became the invisible woman. Finally, Sonya was standing up and owning her own ample, untapped voice and gifts.

Her business advisors were encouraging her to grow her world trade goods business and expand her market, when she wanted to sell it. Her dating explorations were repeating old patterns of attracting narcissistic men who didn't give to her, instead of the conscious, deep soul love she longed for.

"I need more time in the Mystery," she declared one day in our session. Her home was filled with old business goods of her husband's, which she found symbolically taking up space she now needed for herself. "I need more time to integrate Thomas' death. I need to let go of most of his professional things that are cluttering my space. I need to go in, not out right now, and release dating and growing my business. I need more time to retreat and be in the Mystery."

Sonya decided to take off three weeks while her employees ran her import business. She decided to do a personal retreat at home, and go through her home and sell or give away everything that was taking up space and not really representing "her" anymore, including her husband's many business possessions filling the garage. She would select a few treasured things to remember him by, and sell or donate the rest. At the end of our session she was animated and excited, full of vigor for her plan to spend this time integrating further her ending with her old life and creating open space—literally, in her home—to see who she might be next.

Sonya was filled with energy and enthusiasm. She cleared out mountains of boxes of Thomas' possessions, selling those that were valuable, donating more, and keeping a few cherished items. She reorganized her home and set it up as a beautiful, inspiring space with room for her grand piano, artwork, and meditation space. She invited her spiritual community over for a potluck brunch to initiate and celebrate her new space.

Having integrated the recovery of her big Spirit, voice, and power, Sonya was finally able to grieve fully for Thomas. She spent many more sessions allowing tears, loss, and sadness over Thomas' death to finally be felt. Having reclaimed her power, it was now safe to let her loss and grief come through, and express her deep gratitude for the many positive gifts of the marriage.

A new woman emerged in Sonya, and a new outer life began to take shape, mirroring who she had become in her passage through change. She eventually sold her business, studied art, and now has become a professional painter, expressing her own unique voice and vision on canvas with vibrant colors and joy.

*When you don't know which way to go, do nothing.*

≋✣ LAO TZU,
*Tao Te Ching*

## Sitting at the Crossroads

***The Mystery Phase is the perfect time to sit down at the crossroads of your life and wait.*** Give up figuring things out, give up planning. When you do take action, it will be the right action, guided from within. When you give up planning and figuring things out from the level of mind or ego, you are able to turn your life choices over to your own indwelling Spirit, or Higher Self, and wait for instructions. Then extraordinary beauty, like that of the butterfly, has time and space to appear.

*The wisdom of the Divine is always flowing through you, helping you, guiding you.*

You may enact a ritual in nature at the crossroads of several paths, as I have sometimes done in the woods with my "Navigating Change" groups. Speak to the trail you have walked, now behind you, and thank it for its gifts. Burn a cedar and sage bundle, called a smudge stick by Native Americans, as you thank your past and let go of the old trails. Native people believe that burning cedar pulls in positive energy to bless your new beginnings, and burning sage releases the old and clears us. Consider the various ways to move forward, including following a well-trodden path or bushwhacking into the wild unknown. Then sit quietly in meditation, or even lie down in the intersection, and feel where you are in your present time in the Mystery. Take your journal and write a letter to yourself from your Higher Self, letting your inner wisdom flow out to you in words.

The wisdom of the Divine is always flowing through you, helping you, guiding you. You can hear it when you enter the moment—this moment, right here—and give up planning, efforting, and pushing. Then the still, small voice of God can be heard, always waiting to help and guide our lives.

# Being Nobody, Doing Nothing

## Practicing Wu Wei: Finding Fullness in Emptiness

*Give up planning, and the world will be a thousand times better.*

≈✲ LAO TZU,
*Tao Te Ching*

**W**u Wei is the ancient Chinese Taoist practice of doing nothing internally while being engaged fully in the moment you are in, including activity in the world. Wu Wei is the practice of consciously embracing the moment exactly as it is with an open, non-judging mind. In Wu Wei, you allow yourself to be fully immersed in the moment you are in, right here, right now. Nothing needs to change except your presence with the present, and your acceptance of what is going on. In your inner attitude of presence and acceptance, your experience shifts. You consciously suspend planning just for a time and simply just do the next thing.

What a relief to give up planning! Imagine giving up trying to figure out who to be, where to move, what job to take, what career to pursue, what person to see. What a beautiful thing to say to life, and to yourself, "This is it, right here, right now. I breathe deeply. I am here. I am fully present in this day of my life and in my experience of this moment. Nothing external needs to shift for me to find peace. This moment contains in it all the intuition, peace, and wisdom my soul needs in order to find my way. I choose to live this day, and this moment, right here and now, as it is."

The time for big external planning is in Phase 4, "Visionary Beginnings," and the Mystery Phase leads you there naturally. In the Mystery, giving up planning, you still live life. You do things, see people, and take action, but your actions occur spontaneously in response to what's showing up rather than through overt controlling, thinking and effort. An opportunity arises; you are present with yourself, and you feel internally how to meet it, and whether to say yes or no. In Wu Wei, you are living day by day in the Mystery, watching what shows up, and listening to your inner feelings and intuition to choose whether to engage outwardly or not.

*Nothing external needs to shift for me to find peace.*

The soul in transition celebrates having open space to simply be present in the moment. The ego loves critically reviewing the past, especially the faults of others and our own perceived slights or shortcomings, and then dictating the future. In the Mystery Phase, practicing Wu Wei, just for a time you give up moving forward, figuring things out, and trying to control the future. You recognize the fertility and richness awaiting you right here, right now. You are learning to listen to a deeper guidance than that of your rational, logical mind.

The ego makes a great servant, but a terrible boss. It thrives on being out of this moment, working away at plans for the future, and storytelling about the past, all to avoid feeling this moment, right here, right now. Its existence is annihilated by immersion in the moment, so it struggles against what it perceives as doing nothing. But in the grace of the moment you are living within, right here, right now, you can hear how you are being guided from within, and know that you are being taken care of by Spirit.

*Don't just do some-thing—sit there!*

≋✶ ZEN TURNAROUND
OF AN OLD MOTTO

## The Aboriginals by the River

**The aboriginals, and all native people who remain in contact with the teachings of their ancestors, know the territory of Wu Wei—living in the Mystery of the present moment—by heart.** One of my neighbors experienced this when he traveled to Australia on a bus tour. He described observing the Aboriginals one day as the bus rattled down a red dirt road in the Outback.

My neighbor's bus passed a group of aboriginal tribesmen sitting by a stream, silently watching the water flow. He was astounded as he told me the story. "They were just sitting there, doing nothing," he said, amazed. "Nobody was talking. They were doing *absolutely nothing*!" To his Western eyes, accustomed to a society whose ruling value is making things happen in form, their "doing nothing" showed laziness and lack of ambition. However, in the vast quantum field of consciousness in which we are all interconnected, their pure Being by the water may have served the world far more than scores of well-meaning people rushing around trying to force creative, important things to happen.

The aboriginals' very presence, in peace and connection to the soul of the natural world, may have been blessing their world in ways our logical Western minds cannot comprehend. To outer appearances the aboriginals were "doing nothing," but in Spirit doing *everything* of consequence by being fully attuned to the moment, to the sacred energy of All that is.

When you're moving through times of Mystery in your life, pulling back from activity, you open up space to enter into the still, quiet place within where you become a blessing to all on the energetic levels of consciousness. When you train yourself to live more and more in this consciousness of living in the moment, you will be led into your next vision, relationship, job, or place in an almost mystical way. You will know what steps to take in the world, and you will know when to take them.

You will slowly become more like the aboriginals meditating quietly by the river, a blessing of deep presence to the world, while apparently doing "absolutely nothing" for a time. But you will be doing everything internally to allow a new birth of Being to take place inside you. That profound sense of yourself will in turn birth extraordinary new outer creations in your life, sourced by your connection to the gifts of the Moment.

*The problems we face cannot be solved at the same level of thinking we were at when we created them.*

≥* ALBERT EINSTEIN

## Vision-Shifting:
## The Gestational Time between Creations

**We cannot create something new from the template of our old ways of thinking and being.** Our psyche needs empty time to let the new visions gestate and be born. To be in the Mystery requires empty space to let go, and time for listening to your inner self; time for quiet and stillness. The Mystery comes with deep gifts in its hands to transform our lives. If we are too anxious to rush into a new outer job, home, relationship, or life purpose, we can lose the new vision trying to be born.

My friend Meredith called me at the beginning of her month-long seclusion at a famous writers' colony. Writers who are accepted into this wonderful retreat live in cabins in solitude, with no TVs, computers, or phones. Their meals are brought to their cabins, allowing undistracted time to produce work. Meredith had previously spent a joyful, productive, creative month there, and had been excited about returning. But we can't step into the same river twice, and now Meredith was in a different internal place, in her own Mystery.

A highly creative woman who had already produced a formidable volume of her writings, she now faced the common artist-demons of blocked vision and unbending creative darkness. Nothing was coming through. And here she was, self-charged with the mission of creating a body of terrific work in this precious month of time.

"I have no idea what to write about," she said from her cell phone. "I'm just sitting here staring at the woodstove."

"Well, that means you're on your way to a new vision for your work," I said. "You're just not there yet. *Not* knowing what to do is a necessary step before a new kind of vision comes through. Maybe this just isn't the time for creating." She breathed a sigh of relief: how good it is when friends remind us that where we are is just fine, that we are already enough, and that nothing is out of whack in our process.

A few days later, Meredith left the colony, ending her residency early, and drove home to her husband, animals, and the cozy renovated barn where they lived. She realized she truly wanted to be at home with her family in her own nest, and was pushing herself into the seclusion out of a self-flagellating concept of "not doing enough" as a writer, a familiar syndrome of many creative people. As she relaxed into where she was without judging it, all was well.

*Problems cannot be solved on the level at which they occurred.*

➳ MAHARISHI
MAHESH YOGI

A few months later, in its own right time, Meredith emerged from her creative Mystery to discover a totally new vision for her writing. She created a unique series of Goddess books inspired by mythical symbols and images that she loved and had around her home. She published her stories and was well received for the uniqueness of her work. By releasing concepts built on her old style of writing, and letting go into the Mystery of not-knowing what the next vision would be, Meredith allowed space for the new work germinating inside her. At the right time, her new expression stepped forth.

Under pressure, we usually default to what we used to know, and fall back on how we used to do things. Had Meredith pushed herself to compose at the writers' colony, she probably would have continued to write in her old genre and felt creatively unsatisfied. Even worse, once undertaken, the time it would have taken to complete and publish the work done in her old style would have actually *blocked* the emergence of her new vision, still in the cocoon, evolving to wing itself into manifestation. She might never have known what brilliance was getting ready to arrive in its own perfect timing.

*We embrace the chaos so a dancing star can be born.*

*⇒ NIETZSCHE*

## Having Faith in the Hard Times

**The Mystery Phase can feel like sheer chaos, but it's actually a rich, fertile time in which our seeds of new Being, described in Phase 3, are still underground.** The word chaos derives from the ancient Greek *chaos*, meaning gulf, abyss, empty space. The abyss we straddle in the Mystery Phase is, indeed, a time of empty space, a gulf between old and not-yet-born new selves. The loss of who we used to be, and changes in concurrent outer forms of home, career, relationships, and ways of being, can feel like a terrifying spin into sheer chaos. We don't know where to go or how to be. Our legs of outer structures in our lives that once held us up are gone, and we are wobbling. Who are we now? What will we stand on now?

To pass through this channel of time between the old life and the new one not yet born requires great trust and understanding. Have faith: these feelings are natural, and hold gifts in their hands. We can find reassurance from mentors, allies, and wise friends that the ground on which we stand has a deep beauty and presence all its own when enfolded with welcome.

Many decades ago, when I was a young, single ashram resident, I went through one of my passages through the Mystery, but I then had neither the vocabulary nor life wisdom to understand the value of my inner territory. I had recently abandoned old patterns of constantly nice relating, and overly pleasing behaviors that gave me a false sense of security. I recall a wealthy Toronto guest, a frequent visitor to Kripalu, stopping me as I walked down the hall and saying judgmentally, "Don't you ever get tired of smiling?" I was inwardly mad at her (though no doubt smiling) for being so rude and mean, but something in me knew she was right—damn it! An old survival tactic from childhood—keep pleasing others and being nice in order to feel loved and accepted—was disintegrating. Without that outgrown way of being, I had no idea how to be with myself or others. What worth did I have in life if not to please?

During this time, a woman I knew from my workshops at Kripalu Center visited the center and asked to see me. I went to her deluxe private room. She was a high-powered

*Sometimes when things are falling apart, they may actually be falling into place.*

≈ ANONYMOUS

corporate trainer, working in top echelons of the business world, possessed of enormous personal power, dynamism, and presence. Attractive and pulled together, she radiated confidence and surety about herself and her life. I sat on the edge of her bed in my old, white, ashram clothes, feeling like a blob, almost socially catatonic. I did not then know to shield myself from superficial social situations when traveling through my passages through the Mystery. Although usually extroverted and loquacious, I found myself almost unable to speak. Her entire life seemed so pulled together. I felt so disassembled. I skulked from her room and went back to my small ashram room feeling like nobody, a failure beside her glittering persona.

Two years later, this same woman visited Kripalu again and asked for another visit. Now our roles were reversed. I had traveled through that particular passage and was living from a stronger place of authenticity. She looked fragile and lost. She shared that her extreme overwork with corporate clients and insane travel schedule had resulted in a complete collapse on every level. She had suffered a nervous breakdown. Her health had fallen apart. Her body was saying, "We can no longer sustain the persona you are trying to carry in the world. We call you to go inward into the Mystery and rest."

It is a truth that when we do not hear and respond to the needs of the heart and soul, our bodies must carry the split, sometimes communicating our soul's need to retreat and let go through illness, accidents, or breakdowns, forcing us to slow down and hear our inner call for change on a cellular level. When these illnesses or breakdowns happen, it's important to know that we haven't done anything wrong. We are being given an invitation from life to heal and align ourselves more deeply to our true Self.

*Nothing ever goes away until it teaches us what we need to know.*

≋ PEMA CHÖDRÖN

*. . . honor the vast importance of times in the Mystery of our lives when we do not have it all together.*

*When we breathe into the darkness of the Mystery times in our lives, they begin to give off their own special light.*

Fortunately, this woman had a kind mentor, an older gentleman who took her into his oceanfront home. For one year she rested in his guest room, seeing no one but him. She had to reassemble herself from the inside out and move through her own Chaos/Mystery back into a truer sense of Being. She was still finding new grounds of strength and Being in herself, and had come to Kripalu for further healing. I felt honored that she trusted me with her vulnerable story, and I was astonished to think how I had harshly judged myself two years earlier for not having it all together like this woman.

I now know to honor the vast importance of times in the Mystery of our lives when we do not have it all together. Not knowing how to be, what to say, or what to do is a thing of great freedom and joy when allowed in as natural and healthy. The swirling chaos of the cosmos reformulates the gases and black holes into life- and light-giving stars.

We must embrace our own inner feelings of chaos and loss of identity to let the stars of ourselves become born. When we breathe into the darkness of the Mystery times in our lives, they begin to give off their own special light. They tell us what to do next, and how to be. We learn to listen inwardly and pay attention to dreams, feelings, and inclinations that are guiding us forward. Our embrace of times of loss and chaos, when held with honoring and respect, yields a great guiding light that surely guides us forward on our own true paths.

# SECTION 4

# Meditation:
# Following the Guiding
# Light of Spirit

## Giving Up Swimming

*T*o feel the grace of Spirit, we must give ourselves over to being carried by it.* When I was a young seeker at Kripalu Ashram in the 1970's, our community of residents was elated to have our grandfather guru, Swami Kripalu, live among us for five years. This great saint from India had practiced silence and meditation fulltime for the previous eighteen years in India, but broke his silence when he came to the United States in order to teach his grandchildren, as he tenderly called us. For several months, he met with three hundred of us each morning to tell stories, chant his beautiful *bhajans*, or songs, and teach us how to live close to God. One of my favorite stories from his own life concerns a time he nearly drowned.

When Swami Kripalu was a young monk, he once, in an ecstatic state of *samadhi*, or no-mind, wandered into the Indian River Narmada and found himself swept along in a strong current, being pulled under the water. He realized he was drowning. He tried to swim and couldn't keep his head above the water. In desperation he called out for help from his guru, Dadaji, a powerful spiritual master who had died years before. Kripalu heard the unmistakable sound of his guru's voice speak: "STOP SWIMMING. GIVE UP SWIMMING."

He relaxed into the water and surrendered, let go. The water lifted him up and carried him safely to shore. In giving himself over to the grace of God, he was carried along to safety, through no effort of his own. By giving up control and turning his life over to Spirit, his life was saved and he was sustained by the Divine.

We don't know what's possible if we are trying to tread water and humanly control our lives at all times, determining every possible outcome. To feel the grace of Spirit, we must symbolically stop swimming. When we stop struggling and give ourselves over to the intervening presence of Spirit, we are held up and supported, and miracles can occur.

## Hearing Spirit's Guidance through Meditation

*Major breakthroughs and openings often happen when we are doing our inner work, but sustaining the opening is up to us. One simple practice keeps us on track.* I met Daniel, a financial planner with a great big heart, in one of my New England workshops. Daniel had a powerful personal opening in front of the group, a release of an old lack of self-love

*The past is history. The future is a mystery. This moment is a gift. That's why it's called the present.*

≈ AUTHOR UNKNOWN

and a deep healing from his father's harsh judgments, which had belittled his sense of self-esteem and lovability. In a moving sharing, he wept with the group and shared how he had found a great love for himself in the workshop which he had never experienced before. The group loved him and gave him warm and supportive feedback.

At the end of the weekend, Daniel was ebullient in his newfound joy and self-love, radiant with having found a new way of Being in his life, one based on genuine self-esteem and freedom from his previous lack of self-worth. He asked me in the final session how he could maintain this joyful love. I shared what I say in all of my workshops to those wanting to deepen their inner work and connection to Spirit: "Meditate," I said. "Regularly." I taught a bit about meditation practice and some ways to meditate, and encouraged the group to find their own paths that they loved, and practice often.

Four months later, Daniel flew to Santa Fe to take part in a retreat I was leading. Many of his former workshop group members were there as well, so it was a big home-coming. He shared opening night about his backslide into low self-esteem and lack of self-love after the big break-through at the New England workshop. "How is your med-itation practice going?" I asked him teasingly. He looked sheepish. "I haven't meditated at all," he confessed. "Well, you know how you get to Carnegie Hall," I said, citing a lame old joke. "PRACTICE, PRACTICE, PRACTICE." He grinned.

Meditation is one of the most powerful practices you can initiate in your life to produce extraordinary benefits which sustain and guide you in living your life with abun-dant well-being. The regular practice of your chosen form of meditation brings gifts of peace of mind, clear thinking,

*When you feel connected with your Higher Self, you see dilemmas and situations in your life from a fresh perspective that guides you in wise, creative ways . . .*

*Meditation is taking the lamp of your human life and plugging it into the Source.*

emotional well-being, and the sense of being connected with your own Higher Self. When you feel connected with your Higher Self, you see dilemmas and situations in your life from a fresh perspective that guides you in wise, creative ways to live your entire life. My life experience and the work I've done with thousands of others have deepened my belief that meditation is one of the essential gifts of life. I offer teachings and practices for meditation here as a key practice to support you in moving through the Mystery Phase, as well as all of life itself.

Meditation is the practice of being fully present and relaxed in the moment, fully aware, yet completely relaxed, connecting to an abiding sense of peace and well-being that always exists inside of you. The more regularly you practice meditation, the greater the gifts you find in your practice. There is a quality of radiant presence and positive energy often seen in those who meditate regularly, a feeling of calm surrender to what is so, and a clarity of Being that provides new possibilities for creativity and insights.

Meditation is taking the lamp of your human life and plugging it into the Source. That Source energy is always available to us, but we have to choose to plug in our lamps to connect to the light it brings. Meditation is the beautiful time each day when you consciously plug in your lamp. The more you practice, the more the beautiful qualities of meditation—inner peace, relaxation, trust in life, the feeling of being supported by a Higher Power, forgiveness, and love—continue on throughout your day.

We can have big breakthroughs in the presence of gifted facilitators and transformational workshop processes, but the *continuance* of those openings is in our hands. No one I know of lives in an awakened state all the time, needing no conscious spiritual practice to reconnect them to their own Divine nature. Most of us need to create a context for a new way of Being through regular spiritual practice that keeps us connected to our own inner light. Otherwise, that light is shining but we are not connected to it. Without it, we can easily backslide into old beliefs and grooves that once ran our lives. Without meditation, we are not making room in our lives to connect to that inner light of Spirit and to hear the guiding voice of Spirit.

It is a beautiful experience to create a daily ritual of stilling the mind, ceasing outer doing and activity, and entering into a sacred place of quiet attunement within us to return to who we are as spiritual beings. If we are doing all the talking in our lives through excessive planning, figuring out, and controlling our future outcomes, how can God get a word in edgewise?

The meditation practice you choose does not matter. There is no higher or lower path, just the one that you love to do, the one that you feel drawn to, that comes naturally to you. There are many schools and paths of meditation; I favor those that are not rigid with lots of stultifying shoulds and rules; not dogmatic, but based on love, a positive attitude toward yourself and others, and a little humor to keep it real. Your meditation can be just fifteen or twenty minutes in the morning while having tea in your garden. You can create a sacred space you love to be in that supports your sinking into deep quiet.

Once settled in your sacred space, take several long, deep breaths, breathing fully into your belly and inflating your lungs and diaphragm completely, then exhaling all the breath. You can practice yoga, tai chi, chi kung, or another physically meditative art as part of your practice, but when

*The Master doesn't seek fulfillment.*
*Not seeking, not expecting,*
*She is present, and can welcome all things.*

≋ LAO TZU

the physical movement has ceased, allow the energy flow of your physical practice to carry you into stillness for at least ten to fifteen minutes

Once you're settled in your personal sanctuary space, let go of planning and figuring out your life for just this small amount of time. As you enter into the peace of the moment, often illuminating insights and creative answers to presenting problems pop in spontaneously, freed from the constraints of your mind's usual ways of solving problems. I find it helpful to keep a small scratchpad or journal and pen nearby so that these flashes of insight can be jotted down quickly, and then put aside. This allows you not to get mentally distracted trying to remember these important insights or ideas, and return to your meditation, knowing that the note will remind you later on. When you drop into your meditative state of calm, fewer and fewer interrupting thoughts will occur. You will have longer periods of deep peace, immersed in the ever-present beauty of the moment.

*I enter this moment in friendship, with an undefended heart.*

≈≉ SYLVIA BOORSTEIN

## Meditation Potholes: Past-Tripping, Processing, and Projecting

**When our minds wander, it's usually caused by what I call the three P's: past-tripping, processing, and projecting.** It's reassuring to know that literally everyone periodically falls into these potholes in meditation practice, especially at the outset, so you can adopt an attitude of levity and humor about your mental forays out of the moment. Perhaps this is why the Buddha is so often shown smiling.

In *past-tripping*, we review pleasant or painful thoughts about our pasts, which are over. In *processing*, we tell people off, explore hurt feelings, try to figure out challenging situations or dynamics, go over relational and life issues, and struggle to control everything though endless mental review. In *projecting*, we are projecting our thoughts into a future which does not yet exist. We imagine positive fabulous outcomes or fear-based negative outcomes (or both), then process about that! Truly, the human mind is a funny little monkey. Chasing the monkey around our mental cage goes nowhere. We must make a hot cut back to the present. What is a hot cut? Read on.

*Drinking a cup of tea, I stopped the war.*

≈✻ ZEN KOAN

## Meditation Helper: The Hot Cut

*The hot cut helps us keep attuned to our inner peace during our meditation.* In the 1980's, my corporate trainer years, I led retreats with TV executives and their news teams at numerous top stations, including ABC, CBS, and Warner Brothers. It was fascinating to see the master control booths, the complex brains running the news and television shows streaming into our living rooms, and seeing how Doppler weather reports on the evening news consist of the weatherperson standing before a blank blue screen and pointing to what appears on our TV sets as cities, states, and maps, projected onto the screen by technicians. Engineers keep all this running together smoothly, and scores of people are working hard behind each anchor delivering the news to us daily.

One of the television terms I loved was the notion of the hot cut. The hot cut is a technique to keep the viewer engaged on the channel, rather than switching to another channel during the break between shows. As one show ends, the master controller makes a hot cut to the beginning of the next show without commercials or show credits.

Discouraging viewers from diving for the remote to check out other channels, the hot cut keeps the viewer engaged *right here*. This is an excellent practice for reorienting the distracting thoughts that arise during meditation.

I'm meditating and my mind starts reviewing a "commercial" from my past . . . hot cut to the moment with a long, deep breath, bringing myself back to Now. Now I'm thinking of something pleasing or painful someone said and begin processing that . . . hot cut to the moment with a deep breath, returning to Now. An upcoming workshop is not yet designed and I am stressing about the considerable work I have to do . . . hot cut . . . Here We Are. A hot cut is instantaneous. You don't have to figure out *why* you were off on a mental tangent, just gently come back to the present moment.

## Hearing the Guiding Voice of Spirit

***In meditation, you are in training for the game of life.*** For a brief time, you let go of egoistic control and give yourself over to your Higher Power, the greater, infinite Source always waiting to help you out. For just a small amount of time each day, you give up mentally running the show of your life and turn your life over to God. The experience of letting go and being fully present in the moment is exquisite. It is a relief to give up efforting, and let your life, your major decisions, and daily choices be guided by Spirit.

When you are beginning a new relationship, friendship, job, or creative venture, meditation brings you clarity to help you see what is aligned to your greatest good, and what is not. In the calm stillness of meditation, you see your right path forward much more clearly. You can much

*In God I live, and move, and have my Being.*

≋✶ THE BIBLE

more easily disengage at the beginning of a venture or relationship that's not aligned to your greatest good before you sprint down that road too far, thus requiring massive action to get back to your true path.

When you gift yourself with a brief daily period of meditation, even for ten minutes a day, your practice becomes something beautiful you look forward to. Healing occurs on numerous levels. Surprising answers to big issues often drop in when the monologue of the mind is set aside. You find new ways to traverse the opportunities and challenges life is presenting you, and move forward on trails of inner light.

You might like to bring inspiring spiritual books you like to your meditation, and read a few lines before or afterward. Reading uplifting books from any spiritual tradition as part of your meditation practice lets the deeper truths of life touch your soul. Journaling after you meditate, you may find great insights to the life questions you are asking or decisions you are facing coming through. Write down what you hear or sense to be right for you as you listen to the voice of Spirit.

## The Guiding Light in the Darkness: A Night in the Volcanic Crater

*After we exhaust all human possibilities of figuring out how to move forward, we have the choice to give up and let go to a Higher Power.* I learned this lesson in the pit of the extinct Hawaiian volcanic crater called Haleakala in the middle of the night. I was thirty-five years old, only modestly athletic, and had hiked five hours with a forty-five-pound backpack at high altitude down the side of

Haleakala's volcanic crater in Maui, accompanied by my first husband, Paul. Our destination was the crater floor of this extinct volcano.

Shifting from our sea-level camping to ten thousand feet in the clouds overnight, unaware of the demands of extreme altitude adjustment and the rigors of carrying a heavy pack in the intense Hawaiian sun for five hours, I physically collapsed in tears at the bottom of the Sliding Sands trail. My legs literally could not take another step. I was on my edge. I had to breathe and sob and feel completely helpless before finding some gut-strength to carry on to our campsite.

Now Paul and I sat in the night's darkness, campsite pitched and bellies full of ramen, alone in the vast maw of the ancient Hawaiian crater. In the five days spent camping and hiking there, we had seen no other person, just the Hawaiian nene geese and a comical ground squirrel who visited us for handouts at dinner. It was our final night in the crater.

The full moon would be rising in an hour or so. Paul wanted to go over the volcanic fields to watch it rise from some mystical high bluff rising up from the crater floor. I wanted to crawl into my sleeping bag and call it a night. Paul persuaded me to join him.

We set out over the field of black lava rocks. Even with the light of our flashlights beaming, it was nearly impossible to walk over the trail-less expanse of sharp, unforgiving volcanic rocks, a forbidding landscape of cutting black stones forged by once-boiling lava streams. We stumbled and struggled to find our way without falling on the knife edges of the rocks. The time before moonrise was so black that we couldn't see anything.

"Turn off your flashlight," Paul said. What? "Turn off your flashlight. Follow the energy trails left here by the ancient Hawaiians. Let your body lead you. Give up trying, and give up thinking about where to put your feet. Move from your belly, and your body will guide you. You'll feel the energy trails you can't see with your mind. Let yourself be guided."

We knew that the ancient Hawaiians had entered Haleakala's vast miles of volcanic crater floor for a thousand years to enact ceremonies and sacred rituals. Their ancient light trails glistened over the lava rocks in ways the human mind cannot see. We shut off our lights and entered the darkness fully, listening with the intelligence of our bodies.

"Feel the light trails of the Old Ones," Paul coached me. A Scorpio, Paul was always attuned to the deep mysteries of the wilder places we traveled and had the bravado to explore unknown places, an inner trust of the wild and physical that I was just beginning to discover inside myself.

The extraordinary happened: I let go of figuring it out with my mind, and felt the trails connect up with the core energy of my hara, the spiritual center of the body located just below the navel, well known to mystics in the Eastern world. I, the control queen of everything, gave up planning and let go of struggling to move forward, and my body was led on gracefully. I could almost see the trails of light the sacred Hawaiians had left across these mysterious and endless fields of lava rock. Paul felt it too, and we laughed in a kind of contact high. We began to flow quickly and easily over the sharp, uneven rocks and playfully danced our way to the top of a bluff in the lava field, overlooking vast seas of the black pointy rocks. We let ourselves go into the night mysteries.

I was exhilarated with the discovery that I was led in the dark by letting go to a higher power. Paul and I sat down on

*To go in the dark with a light is to know the light.*
*To know the dark, go dark. Go without sight,*
*And find that the dark, too, blooms and sings,*
*And is traveled by dark feet and dark wings.*

≈ WENDELL BERRY,
*"To Know the Dark"*

the edge of the high cliff of lava. The night horizon took on a dim illumination at the crest of the field. It grew brighter and brighter. The full moon rose, and all that was blackness before was suddenly illuminated in near-daylight. We meditated with the spirits of the ancient Hawaiians in their sacred fields of light.

A miraculous breakthrough occurred when we hiked up out of the crater the next morning. While I had now adjusted to the high altitude, the trail ascending the crater wall was steep, a challenging climb uphill in the hot Hawaiian sun. But I was now moving powered by a new vitality, energized by Spirit and not purely from my own physical effort. I literally ran up many sections of the trail with my pack on while Paul laughed in pleasure at my transformation. The energy I had discovered of allowing Spirit to lead me seemed to carry my feet uphill from the bottom of the crater to the top rim of Haleakala.

In the dark times in our lives, in the Mystery Phase of each life change we navigate, there is always a way to proceed step by step, moment by moment by turning to our indwelling Spirit or Higher Self. This doesn't happen on its own. We need to *choose* it, *turn* to it, and *then listen* to what comes through. What comes through can be so brilliant and out of the box that it astounds our limited, figuring-things-out minds, the minds that only see what we used to know, not the vast new possibilities offered by Spirit.

As we go in the dark with a light, we can only see what the light shines on. But when we trust the beauty of wisdom offered by surrendering to the dark, another kind of guidance can come through, and show us the way, step by step.

*This is it.*

≋✤ LAO TZU

## Living in the Moment

***Your conscious passage through the Mystery leads you to your true Being.*** Your true Being shines forth only in the moment, not in a future plan. Even when you plan something wonderful for your future, when you get to that moment, all you've got is YOU—your Being, the presence you have once you're standing there inside of that moment, which once you dreamed about and now you have created. Now here you are. This is it!

When you are moving through the Mystery Phase, you are learning to live more from the moment and less from your future plans. You are learning a new way of Being that will later make everything you create, do, and enact infinitely more fulfilling because it will be connected to the Source of your inner Being. In the Mystery Phase, you're discovering ways to live a life of magnificence and purpose, learning how to move from moment to moment, life experience to life experience, and to move forward with trust in the goodness of your life. You learn to feel connected to Spirit.

Your feeling of connection with the light in all things changes the way you create in the next phases of change. Your spiritual connection is always right here, before you and within you, in the embrace of here and now, in the breath, in nature, in meditation, and in the moment. When you learn to live from your connection with Spirit, you see the light, the good, and the gifts in all things and all people. Life itself becomes increasingly joyful because you are living in it, not in your future plans. You will make plans, but live in the Now. When it's time to take action, you will move forward rooted in inner strength and energized by your Source, your inner guidance.

*When you learn to live from your connection with Spirit, you see the light, the good, and the gifts in all things and all people.*

Every life experience serves you. Retreating and reflecting for a time between forms, and tracking your own inner guidance, you gain trust in the goodness of your life episodes. You see how everything you've been through has awakened you. Everything you've used consciously has helped you open your heart, find your strength, and grow in your connection to Spirit. You discover that, in the moment before you, liberated from worrying about the future or pondering your past, all is well. Your life is unfolding exactly as it should for your highest good. You have made no mistakes. Your life's many unfolding events have all played their role in your evolutionary joy.

Being in the Mystery of your life, your new way of being alive has space to be born. You are learning to greet what comes to the door of each moment as an old friend arriving with a gift in his hands. Take a deep breath, open the door and say, "Welcome!"

*You have journeyed well through*
*the Mystery Phase of your transition. Now*
*new life is stirring, new values emerging, and a*
*new way of Being is calling you.*
*You are entering Phase 3 of Navigating Change:*
*"The Phoenix Rises: Emergence of New Being."*
*Prepare to spread your wings and lift off!*

# PHASE 3

# THE PHOENIX RISES

*Emergence of New Being*

# PHASE 3

⚜

# The Phoenix Rises:
# Emergence of New Being

As you've journeyed through the Phases of Change in this book, a miraculous transformation has been taking place. You have been changed. A new you, with a new way of living your life, is being born. The discovery of your truest values for living your life and the courage to live from a new way of Being are coming alive. You are entering Phase 3, "The Phoenix Rises."

You may awaken with a new vigor and vitality. You may feel a new life surging in you. You want to charge forward! Inspiring new ideas for your life, work, and expression may be showing up. You may feel a confident, playful, excited energy surging into your spirit as you sense your potential to create a new life for yourself. You have done your inner work, and a newfound joy and emerging vision are surfacing. But as you prepare to launch your next steps, first clarify the essential ingredient that determines your true fulfillment and happiness: having a clear *Being Vision* for your life.

**In Phase 3, "The Phoenix Rises,"** you'll learn why it's vital to know your new Vision for Being before deciding what you do next. You'll recreate your life from the inside

*i thank You God for this*
*   amazing*
*   day: for everything*
*   which is natural*
*   which is infinite which*
*   is yes*
*(i who have died am*
*   alive again today,*
*   and this is the birth*
*   day of life and of love*
*   and wings) . . .*
*(now the ears of my ears*
*   awake and*
*   now the eyes of my*
*   eyes are opened)*

⚜ e.e. cummings,
*   "i thank You God"*

out, from your Being, which is the way you live, feel, and approach Being in your life. You will be guided step-by-step in creating a heartfelt, personal, passionate Being Vision as the foundation for your life. You will then learn steps to practice living from your Being Vision, transforming your experience of your life. Finally, you'll read inspiring stories of others finding new Being, illustrating how they positively shifted their outer lives by putting Being first.

**In Phase 4, "Visionary Beginnings,"** you'll build on your Being Vision to create your new expression in your life. Your Being Vision becomes the foundation for all you will express and do going forward.

## Phase 3: The Phoenix Rises includes:

# Rising from the Ashes: Your New Self

## A New You Arising

The ancient Egyptians worshipped the phoenix, a mythological bird who rises from the ashes of offerings made on a sacrificial fire. You have been burning up old limiting thoughts and feelings about your life in the fire of change. You've let go of much of what no longer serves you, and released outgrown forms. You've forgiven those you felt had wronged you, freeing your Spirit. These are your offerings at the sacred fire of your life. Your offering up and letting go of the old and outgrown in your life generates the ashes from which your phoenix of new Being rises.

Today, you are a different person from the woman or man you were before this journey of change. Ask yourself, and then write down or draw the answers to these questions: Who am I now? What is changed in me? Who is the new person in me arising from the ashes of my change journey?

As you answer these questions, you're discovering a new you who is being born. Welcome her in, welcome him in. Your answers will lead you to your Being Vision in these pages. When your Vision for Being is clear, it becomes your inner compass guiding all you choose, activate, and create next in your life. Everything you accomplish and draw to you next will be the outer reflection of who you are, of your new way of Being, and the new consciousness being born in you.

Knowing who you are now and what state of Being you wish to live from will guide every path you embark on and every choice you make from here on. Your new Being will be expressed in all you do.

## An Attitude of Gratitude: Starting from Enough

***There is a secret inner practice that instantly shifts our states of mind and feelings.*** This practice lies at the heart of creating a fantastic, fulfilling life. No matter what is happening on a given day of challenges, or how funky we may be feeling, or how much we're complaining about some problem *du jour*, this practice changes our state of Being in the twinkling of an eye. And it's so immediately available and simple it may seem not important at first glance. But experiment and see the results for yourself.

The simple, secret practice is *gratitude*: gratitude for what's happening right now, gratitude for all the good in our lives today, noticing how full our cups are and taking a moment to express our gratitude, whether silently or out loud.

Suddenly, although nothing external has changed at all, our outlooks have radically changed. We begin to feel more buoyant and upbeat. Our problems still exist out there in the world around us, but now we see the potential solutions and surprising opportunities hidden within them. We let go of whining and being in the victim position, and instead empower ourselves to see our lives in new ways that actually bring good out of apparently bad circumstances.

What's wonderful about your life right now? Say it out loud. What creative opportunities are sitting in the hands of today's presenting problems or challenges? Notice them and express thankfulness for them. Besides what's facing you right now, what's working about your life? Who loves you who is alive and present for you? What health advantages do you have that you aren't even noticing? Look around you at the life you have manifested and see the good. Say it to yourself, "I am grateful for . . . ."

Sometimes just reframing my outlook on a troublesome or scary or difficult day changes how I feel in that day, instantly changing how I deal with what's happening. Saying to myself, "Today is a wonderful day!" I suddenly notice what actually *is* wonderful. Instantly my outlook is transformed. My focus of thought is lifted above my own petty issues or personal insults or perceived difficulties—most of which are the result of my interpretations anyway—into the world of love and abundance that actually surrounds me.

Anyone can notice and complain about what's wrong: that's how many people trudge through life. But to notice what's right and feed it, speak about it, and be aware of it in the face of life's challenges is genius. Gratitude shows our empowerment to create our experiences the way we choose, not living as the victims of outer events.

Practicing gratitude, I suddenly feel rich. My life feels full of love, and I remember that I have so much to appreciate here and now. What I focus on becomes strengthened and expanded, because that which we focus upon expands and grows.

Start with all that is well in your life, and let gratitude bring you into Being. As you pay attention to the countless gifts in your current life, you will feel filled up. Your heart will open to see how abundant and good your life is right now. You will be living from enough. In this expanded state of gratitude, you will be standing in your essential wholeness: the perfect place from which to move forward.

*If the only prayer you said was thank you, that would be enough.*

— Meister Eckhart

## Gratitude and Being When Things Fall Apart

It's easy to practice gratitude and flow in a state of Being when the externals of our lives are going well, but what about when things fall apart? These challenging times are when our new beginnings are just around the corner, and we help them emerge by practicing Being and gratitude.

When I was 31, I took a year's sabbatical from Kripalu to go to Alaska. In those years, Kripalu was still an ashram, and all of us on staff worked without income. I had no savings to finance my big adventure except for $200. I'd saved from illustration work I'd done in my spare time. I needed to break out, take a big risk and go for it. I couldn't watch my life go by with many dreams lingering inside me. I thought that I could live week-by-week on the modest salary the center offered. A friend loaned the money for a one-way airline ticket. The center director, Paige, invited me to co-rent a house with her high up in the mountains and I accepted. I arrived in a blizzard in mid-November to start my new life.

When we embark on a huge new life vision, we need to take action knowing that we will probably have some hard times, and that hard times do not necessarily mean we've made a mistake. After a few weeks on my new job, my support systems vanished. Paige told me that the center would be closing for a few weeks during the holidays while she went to Hawaii, and that I would be without income for that time. I was borrowing her friend's car which also suddenly became unavailable. I had no way to purchase a car, so this meant that I'd be alone in our house, up in the Chugach mountains.

After Paige left for Hawaii, and I paid the rent, I had $20. left. I had no bank account, no car, no friends, no way to get into Anchorage to buy food, and no money with which to buy it. I didn't have family I could call and say, "I'm in a jam. Can you wire me $500?" It was a critical turning point in my life. Was I going to run back to the ashram and be codependent on it for the rest of my life? Or was I going to dig in and find out what was possible?

I decided, amidst tears, fears and sleepless nights: "I'm not moving. I'm staying right here." I decided, "I'm going to be on retreat here in my house in the mountains. I have a big bag of brown rice. I've fasted a lot, and I can fast on that. I have some dark beer. Each night, I can light a fire, listen to my Pat Metheny tape, and have one beer." This was my evening ritual, snow falling outside, fire crackling, jazz playing, and the peace of the winter stars and northern lights keeping watch over the mountains. To this day, when I hear the sounds of Pat's *New Chautauqua* album, I'm transported to sitting alone by the fire, drinking a dark beer and writing in my journal in the Alaskan starlit night.

Once I accepted what was happening as a great opportunity, I had an extraordinary time on retreat in those mountains. I had my ashram bedroll, and a little altar, a board on two bricks with little sacred objects. I made art. I meditated. I did yoga. Every day, I went out when the sun shone for those few precious hours and took walks in the mountains. On my walks, a neighbor's collie always ran over to join me. I checked his name tag: his name was Spirit. In all ways, Spirit was walking with me every day.

To stay in Alaska under these circumstances seemed impossibly difficult at first. I had to go through loneliness, face poverty, feel isolated, and watch my security of job, car, income and roommate unexpectedly evaporate after just one month. But there was a gem of gold waiting inside my circumstances. I would have lost so much if I had given up when everything seemed to fall apart, a powerful life lesson in trust and faith.

## The Universe is on the Phone

One morning, I was doing my morning meditation and suddenly felt deep gratitude for God's abundance. My heart welled up with the great love of the universe surrounding me, even in my challenging circumstances. I thanked God for His abundance in my life. I wanted to do something to express my abundance, so from my remaining twenty dollars I wrote a check to Kripalu's Development Department for five dollars as a tithe. No one there knew what was happening in my life. I walked down our winding dirt road to the mailboxes and mailed the check. Then I let it go.

I had three dreams: to be a writer, to be a teacher, and to be an artist, the three things I still do today. Later that day, the phone rang. I hardly knew anyone in Alaska; who could it be? On the phone was the owner of the printing company who did the program brochures for Paige's workshop center where I was employed. In my first month there, I had designed and illustrated the center's program brochure. "I like your drawings, and we need an artist here," he said. "Would you like to work for us fulltime as an artist?" He offered me significantly more money than I was making at the workshop center. I said, "Yes! I accept!" thanking God for this abundance coming into my life. Now I had employment as an artist!

Still later that day, after my walk with Spirit, I had another phone call, this time from Maui. The person calling was Paul Deslauriers, a man who had once lived at Kripalu and now ran an oceanographic consulting company in Anchorage. I had moonlighted at night doing technical editing for his company in my first month to help cover my moving costs. He said, "I like the way you edited my technical journals. Could I offer you a job at my company as a writer?" His salary was also much higher than I was currently earning at the workshop center. I said, "Yes!"

By getting on the phone with God, but without making one human call, I now had two wonderful job offers doing work I love. I resigned from Paige's workshop center, took both jobs, and worked mornings as an artist, and afternoons doing technical editing. I lunched between my two jobs at a health food cafe where I filled up on soup and bread. Paul loaned me $1000. for a car, which I repaid in three months. I named the car Dadaji, or Grandfather, after one of my lineage of gurus, and felt Dadaji was taking care of me in the form of an old Dodge Dart with bare tires, watching over me as I drove safely through the ice and blizzards of an Alaskan winter.

My oceanographic editing job quickly evolved into my being a fulltime professional trainer for Paul's company. We began working on a contract in the remote Tlingit village of Yakutat, a traditional village in the Gulf of Alaska accessible only by boat or private plane. My clients were local tribal government officials, nice local men in rusted out pickup trucks who were commercial fishermen by day, and the chiefs of the Tlingit tribe, whom I interviewed at the local bar.

From sitting alone in my house without income, money, or a car, I was now being flown by our client's private jet with Paul over the Wrangell glacier to Yakutat. We interviewed Gulf of Alaska fishermen and oil company executives, visited the ancient burial sites, sacred hunting grounds and spiritual lands of the Tlingits escorted by tribal members, all as part of our work to create a training program to sensitize oil rig workers to the Tlingit Indian culture, a federally mandated program for which we were hired. Imagine if I had turned and run home when things seemed to fall apart? What I would have lost, what opportunity given up?

As we travelled, worked and created together, my platonic friendship with Paul became a romance in the beautiful lands of Alaska. We eventually returned to the Berkshires and later married for ten years. My whole outer life changed into a vastly new expression from the life I'd led only two months prior at Kripalu.

What came out of my experience was the most important teaching of my life: *that there is spiritual help and abundance surrounding us at every moment.* It's there when we can't see it and circumstances appear hard. We can access it only if we align ourselves with gratitude and good and do the spiritual practices that put us in touch with our Being, our Higher Self. Spirit is always right next door to us, ready when called to walk at our side. It might look like a fuzzy collie, it might be invisible, it might come as guidance to give when we feel broke or find gratitude for the good we do have. But no matter what our outer circumstances are presenting, Spirit is always showing us the way home to ourselves, ultimately bringing us new opportunities to bless us on our path going forward.

*... there is spiritual help and abundance surrounding us at every moment.*

# Being Precedes Doing

## Know Who You Are Before Figuring Out What to Do

Outside of our old summer cottage on Massachusetts' Lake Mahkinac, the lake waters shimmered in the morning light. I had scheduled this day for a vision coaching retreat with Zane, a former corporate client, a man who had grown to be a cherished friend.

A decade earlier, in my corporate career, I had worked for Zane as a consultant when he was the owner of a corporation. He was now in a different stretch of the road. Zane had just closed his company and was seeking his next step in life.

With a formidable creative mind that went a million miles an hour with ideas, inspirations, and directions, Zane outlined numerous creative plans and doing visions for the next phase of his life, wondering which fork in the road to travel next, but finding no clear answer.

By the end of the afternoon, Zane had run through all of his dreams and plans for various new businesses. Nothing felt completely right; nothing grabbed his passion as the

*"I have to figure out who I want to BE before I know what I want to DO."*

perfect next step. As we sat together in the fading light, finally there were no more words. He gave up figuring it out; I gave up efforting to help. Our mutual work, our struggle to find answers for him in our roles as client and coach, seemed to dissolve into just being together, here and now, in the moment. Peace settled over my small cottage and rested in the space between us. I was simply sitting with an old friend.

Zane looked at me silently. Then he said: "Christine, I just got it."

"Got what, Zane?"

"I have to figure out who I want to BE before I know what I want to DO."

I never forgot that moment.

Two years later, Zane and I had dinner. I asked him what he had done since our day together.

"Molly and I let go of just about everything we had and the life we'd created. We sold our furnishings and our home and reinvented ourselves. We live in Nantucket now. I'm working with emerging writers in developing their creative voices. We've bought an old farmhouse. The old life was good. It was a match for who I'd been then. But I had grown and changed."

In the space between life chapters, we need to take time to discover who we are now before we can truly know which way to go. When we recognize who we've become, our Being leads us forward and births the new.

## Pain in Paradise: Gauguin's Tale

It was 1969, and I was sitting on the floor in the University of Delaware library art stacks in my flower child uniform: faded jeans with shredded hems, dirty bare feet, and black dancer's leotard. I hungered to paint like Paul Gaugin. Instead of living in boring red brick Rodney dorms in provincial Newark, Delaware, I wanted *the life* of Paul Gaugin. I'd never been off the East Coast, and his swirling colors, aqua seas, and sensual, beautiful women called me like sirens to abandon the secure life of my college-kid boat and take a leap.

In a premonition of the life I would lead many decades later in Hawaii, I wanted to live on an island and paint and be free like Paul. My eighteen-year-old self pondered the title of one of his final paintings, a triptych of young and old women, mothers with children, swelling teal blue seas, and towering coconut palms. "What are we? Where did we come from? Where are we going?" I knew these questions by heart, but I had not yet answered them. I did not then know that seeking the answers would form the quest of my entire life.

I read about Paul's life, eager to learn how he created his idyllic existence. I was shocked to read that Gaugin died of syphilis, penniless, alone, in the squalor of his Tahitian hut. What happened? Gaugin left behind his family and children and a soul-stifling job as a financial officer in France, and ran away to Polynesia. His life looked exciting, artistic, free, and passionate on the outside. He changed every outer form in his life and wove a fantastical dream life of painting in paradise. How, I wondered, did it come to pass that his life ended as it had?

We carry our wounds with us everywhere we go, until we finally address and heal them. As I researched Gauguin's life, I saw that he had changed the outer forms of his life, but not who he was inside. Gauguin's unfaced suffering, the

*"What are we? Where did we come from? Where are we going?"*

⇒ TITLE OF ONE OF GAUGUIN'S FINAL PAINTINGS

ambition and unfulfilled longing for worldly success, the depression that had haunted him in France, all went with him to Polynesia. He created a big doing vision for his bohemian soul, but the inner peace and Being to support that vision was not in place. Poignantly, like his friend Van Gogh, his paintings did not find significant commercial acclaim until after his death, a reminder to enjoy the work we do *in the process of* making it, in case worldly success is not in the cards.

Gaugin gave us a mighty lesson in the title of one of his last paintings, a title that emblemizes his life. At the end, he was asking, "What are we? Where have we come from? Where are we going?" His gift of these questions touches me. They are questions from his heart, perfect questions to consider for ourselves in our own regenerating passages into lives of new meaning and expression.

*Success is not the key to happiness. Happiness is the key to success. If you love what you are doing, you will be successful.*

❀ THE BUDDHA

## Creating by Being:
## The Raven Shows the Way

Ingrid showed up for our first coaching session in a black business outfit with gold jewelry, an unusual sight in artsy, casual Santa Fe. "I just moved to Santa Fe from NYC to change my life," she began. "I am a life coach, and have an advanced life coaching certificate with one of the nation's top coaching institutes. I have my business plan to launch my practice here all drawn up. But I'm frustrated. I'm not getting clients yet. I came for help."

Ingrid's plan was a sound one, smart and organized and well thought out, but her map for action left no room for being a woman in a brand new life, having time in the Mystery, and finding out what new expression wanted to be born in her.

In only four months in town, Ingrid had set up an extensive website, had articles printed in prestigious online journals, joined numerous local business networking organizations, and arranged to speak for the chamber of commerce. I felt self-rejecting as I listened to all she'd put in place. I really dislike marketing, and hadn't done any of these things, except create a website, which to me was artistic and fun, like writing an illustrated love letter to people I like. "And I haven't gotten one client from any of it," she said, repeating, "I'm so frustrated!"

"Let's take a few long deep breaths together, and just be fully present to all you are experiencing, without judging it," I said. We closed our eyes for a moment and breathed together, relaxing. "Let yourself stop fighting what is. Stand and breathe and be fully right here in the midst of all that you are experiencing. Welcome it as a friend, not an enemy." Tears welled up in Ingrid's brown eyes and slid down her cheeks. Her face softened. She sipped some tea and looked at me vulnerably.

"Who am I?" she asked. "Why am I really here? Where do I fit in?" Now we had arrived at the real questions, the true questions we all need to ask, the same ones Gauguin had asked at the end of his life. I also can get willful, controlling and forcing things when I'm not trusting life, getting temporarily disconnected from my Being. I know firsthand how unpleasant it is to struggle to force things I think I need into being. I respected the ground she was tracking.

"Close your eyes. Let go of everything your mind says you should be doing right now. Allow an image to float up in your mind symbolizing your true Self," I said.

"I see a raven. I want to be a bird, a raven! I hear the cry of the raven. I want to fly free on the air currents and soar. I have always loved ravens."

*Stand and breathe and be fully right here in the midst of all that you are experiencing. Welcome it as a friend, not an enemy.*

*. . . go to a place you love in nature with your journal, and ask your inner raven to write you a letter . . . .*

"What are the qualities of a raven to you?" I asked.

"Keen eyesight—the raven sees everything with big vision. Soaring high over the trees. It has a loud call, a strong voice it sounds out to the world."

Symbols that arise in our minds are guideposts pointing us toward our truths. "Here is your homework for the next week," I said. "Listen to the sound of the raven online. Look for ravens in your walks. Then go to a place you love in nature with your journal, and ask your inner raven to write you a letter about your voice and your call in the world.

"One more thing: for the next week, no doing plans, no action plans to move your career forward in the way you think of it. This inner Being practice is what is called for right now."

"Wow, that is hard!"

"Why?"

"Because then I'll have to relax!" We laughed.

"Ingrid, you have to know who you are before you can figure out what your voice is," I said. "And you need to know your Being and your voice before you figure out what outer life choices best express them. You've done plenty of doing and action here, and nothing has resulted that pleases you. Let's try a new approach—Being."

We hugged goodbye in my doorway. The Santa Fe sun shone in through my French doors, illuminating her face.

"I'm supposed to be going to a business networking meeting right now," she frowned. This explained the elegant black outfit. "But I never get any work out of those meetings. Everyone's just trying to build their own businesses."

"What do you *want* to do?" I asked.

"Go home and cook for my family and hang out with them. I love to cook, and I love being with them."

"Go home then, and enjoy your evening with your family." And she did.

Ingrid showed up for her next session in jeans and a hand painted t-shirt awash with rose, chartreuse, and gold. She plopped down on my white client couch and pulled her raven letter out of her hand-tooled, brown leather bag.

"Stand up!" I asked. "Stand up and read your guidance out loud."

On her feet, Ingrid embodied her powerful woman with much to give and much to say to the world. Her raven-voice was straight and true.

"Soar free, Ingrid," she read. "Rest in the wind currents. They will carry you where you need to go. From on high you will see your territory and know where to land. Call out. Sound your cry. Fly free in your life with me, your inner raven, your free, soaring woman." She beamed at me. It was a Phoenix rising moment for Ingrid. Her inner raven was soaring high.

"Fantastic, Ingrid!"

"What do you love?" I asked one day, as Ingrid was feeling drawn to find her new expression.

Her response was immediate, passionate. "I love serving women. I want to bring women together to explore what we need in our growth. I want to empower women to have their own voices and live from their own big Selves." Exactly the work Ingrid had now done on herself. She was walking her talk and now ready to move into a new expression.

Ingrid decided to create gatherings in self-esteem and empowerment for women. Once she clarified her new vision, a perfect gathering space appeared with a garden, couches in a circle for cozy talks, and a kitchen for coffee and snacks. Thirty women showed up for her first gathering. By first addressing her own need for Being, she touched a need in the community. She was doing work she loved. Her raven was on the wing.

If you are forcing something to happen, step back. Do something body and Spirit oriented. Take a long walk in nature, breathing deeply. Swim. Dance. Be. For a time, let go of accomplishing something and go enjoy your life as it is, right now. In this refreshed state, new answers and directions can appear. *Be* instead of *do*, and you will be guided into your next outer expression when you are ready.

## Coming Home to Being

***We live in our states of Being, not in our houses.*** When we love and value our peace and joy first, our material lives become the outflow of our vibrational states. The right homes, the perfect partners and jobs all show up at the right time as the natural outpicturing of our Being. The key is to have an intentional Being Vision and practice living from it every day. Remembering our Vision for Being is especially important when we're creating a physical home.

Our Santa Fe Couples' Vision Group members were sitting round our small living room, fat gold candles burning on the old Moroccan coffee table, their light flickering on the overhead viga-and-latilla ceiling of our house. Kenn and I were facilitating this weekly group to coach couples in creating visions for their relationships. To my left sat Adrian, a man with wavy silver hair. Beside him, his wife Celeste sat attentively.

From the outset, this couple was in breakdown; Adrian slumped resignedly in his chair, as Celeste criticized him often when he spoke. They told their tale of woe in the group circle, impressing me with their honesty and realness.

"Last year, we took part in a weeklong 'Live Your Destiny' retreat led by a famous seminar leader. We were all guided to create a dynamic new life plan—what Christine calls a Doing Vision. We created this huge plan for a new dream life in Santa Fe, which we really thought would make us happy. We accomplished every single step of our plan.

"We bought an old ranch outside of Santa Fe. We rebuilt the house, then, with help from a local farmer, renewed the orchards by the river. We planted beautiful gardens. Celeste decorated the house in classic hacienda ranch style. She completed her degree in art therapy and set up her practice in an historic downtown office. Everything we envisioned at the workshop was put into place, just as we wrote it down at the workshop.

"But we've been absolutely miserable!" This we could see. Their suffering affected us all. None of us could judge them, as we all knew the terrain of focusing on achieving things instead of being at peace and living first from our inner happiness and well-being.

That night after group, in our bedroom, Kenn and I joked about our own argumentative, stressed-out, past house renovations, noting how hard it is to stay loving when you're constantly schlepping to Home Depot and exhausted from working twelve-hour days overseeing construction. He wryly quoted the *Course in Miracles*: "A thousand homes you've tried to build, and all you ever built was hell." We both wanted to help this couple, good people who were stuck in blaming each other for the failure of their artfully crafted material life to produce genuine love and happiness.

As the couples in the group developed their visions for their marriages, we explored the vision trap of focusing all our attention on outer forms—the house, the furnishings, the gardens, the trips—without clarifying our Being Visions. Every couple then found a private spot in our home in which to curl up together, write down their

Being Visions, and share them. The love between partners was tangible as they sat closely together, sharing heart to heart about what really mattered most in their lives. And none of it was about the externals.

Adrian and Celeste returned to our circle holding hands, excitement rolling off them. "We've just had a big breakthrough!" Adrian exclaimed. "We got to see how we went off course and fell into this hole. At our 'Live Your Destiny' retreat, none of the speakers addressed Being. We were completely focused on doing, on all the great things we wanted to manifest. We thought these things would make us happy. We've been miserable.

"Now we have a new plan—a Being Vision, first with ourselves, and then with each other; a vision that's based on love, peace, and respect—not on our outer achievements. We're starting all over in our marriage today with our Being Vision to guide our decisions. We feel closer than we have in a long period of making things happen."

Two years later, Celeste called me to check in from a beach campground. She was bubbly and her voice sounded younger. "Adrian and I are camping on the beach in California and having a ball just hanging out together every day. We are rediscovering the couple we were when we first fell in love.

"We sold the Santa Fe ranch. We realized it was just too much work and wasn't making us happy. We've bought an RV and have been traveling around, just being kids in love together, for this entire year. We have no plans. We're not doing anything but loving each other and enjoying wherever we are. We are really living the Being Vision we created in group. Eventually we'll settle down in a new place and create a new life there. But for now, this is exactly what we needed, and we are so happy."

# SECTION 3

# Creating Your Being Vision

## Creating Your Life from Soul and Heart

Your Being Vision is your personal life guide, aligning your actions and choices to your deepest personal values. It brings you back home to yourself; it reminds you to live and move from your truth. Living in Being, you will create and manifest wonderful outer things in your life, but you will move from the center of who you are and make doing choices that support your Being.

What we create and do expresses our consciousness, our Being. Knowing who you want to be in essence and practicing living from your highest values as a human being is the surest path to create a life you love. When you do this, your life shines. Things unfold in surprising ways that often surpass what you thought was possible. You become a magnet for good because you know who you are and are practicing living from your own Higher Self. Your starting point is your Being Vision.

*And now here is my secret, a very simple secret:*
*It is only with the heart that one can see rightly; what is essential is invisible to the eye.*

≋✦ ANTOINE
DE SAINT-EXUPÉRY,
*The Little Prince*

My entire life path, my work, my profession, and all I have manifested in the world have been built on one heartfelt desire I discovered at age twenty—a Being Vision for my life. My Being Vision was to awaken spiritually and live in love and peace. I wanted to find my guru and live in a spiritual community with beautiful, loving people practicing meditation and yoga and sharing a spiritual life together.

Without guru-shopping, when I was twenty-two I serendipitously met Yogi Amrit Desai and I moved into his Kripalu Yoga Ashram. In the naiveté of a twenty-two year old, I thought I'd stay for three months and become enlightened. Instead I stayed for thirteen years and left more fully human.

After several years, I was asked to counsel guests and residents and give Kripalu workshops on the road, a terrifying, exhilarating prospect for me at twenty-six. Gifted therapists and teachers in the Kripalu community mentored and supervised me and others, as we served Kripalu's growing tidal wave of guests and residents. I was glued to every word Yogi Desai said each night in our gatherings, called *satsangas,* and I watched him counsel and facilitate thousands of people bringing their deepest problems, fears, and challenges for help. I'd write down his words, his answers, and my observations of how he went straight to the heart of each person's need. I was modeling from my spiritual teacher how to counsel and teach people. It was the training of my life for what has become the work of my life.

Life at Kripalu in those early years was not for the faint of heart, although it was definitely for the heartful. "It's the love," we joked as carloads of guests poured up the driveway for our expanding offerings of weekend workshops and retreats. Living at Kripalu was dancing in the fire of love, in nonstop personal and spiritual growth. We all burned through layers of fear and ego, awakening in the process to the great and good in ourselves and others. And we learned that from our lineage of gurus.

Our grandfather guru, Swami Kripalu, for whom the Kripalu path is named, had a Being Vision of his own which was our guiding philosophy: "*Vasudhaiva Kutumbakam,*" or, "The world is one family." We practiced living from this Spirit, however imperfectly. His core teaching formed the heart of how I learned to make choices and live in the world.

*The world is one family.*
≋ SWAMI KRIPALU

We have to keep our lofty spiritual ideals grounded in being what I call "plain old human beings." My best friend Kate and I escaped sometimes for pizza and beer or breakfast and coffee at a nearby café to laugh, gossip, and have fun. And when the time came, I married, moved out into the world, and carried what I'd learned from my life of Being into being a corporate trainer and consultant, and then income streamed in. In retrospect, I see that life took care of me because I placed Being first. I am grateful for that passionate, idealistic, twenty-two-year-old woman who followed her heart and knew her Being Vision, and put it first. She birthed the woman I am today.

Your Being Vision is going to birth who you become as well. It is an inner vision statement you create that defines the values, feelings, and consciousness from which you want to live your life. It expresses the true inner purpose of your life. Your Being, not what you do, is your gift to the world. It is the real contribution you make to the world, regardless of your work or expression. Your Being Vision is a personal affirmation, a statement of Being, declaring the values, purpose, and heart with which you want to live.

The following section guides you in creating your Being Vision. After this section, you'll learn tools to embody and practice your Being Vision so that it becomes part of your thinking, feeling, and life. Here are the directions to initiate your Being Vision.

## Creating and Writing Down Your Being Vision

***Creating your Being Vision is a deep, expansive personal exercise.*** You will be attuning to what really matters in your life experience and creating the person you wish to be as you write. What you envision, you start to become with each thought. As you get in touch with your Being Vision, then practice it, you take charge of your consciousness and life. Your outer life mirrors back who you are becoming, with opportunities, people, and moments that support what you believe to be true about you. We'll explore this in Phase 4, "Visionary Beginnings."

To begin, create a quiet time when your energy is fresh and clear and you feel rested and open. Be alone and undisturbed, away from computers, phones, cell phones, and other interruptions. If you wish to, go into nature or your garden with your writing and possibly some art materials.

Have a beautiful journal or writing papers and pen that you love, which honor the importance of your own inner work. My own writing pen has a lapis stone on the top, the stone which affirms voice and speaking truth, and strengthens the throat chakra. I only use it for journaling or book writing. Create a sacred space in the way that calls you: perhaps draw a card from a divining deck you love, sing a song that carries your essence, or say a prayer that has meaning for you. Then breathe and meditate for a few minutes. Connect to your soul and ask your Higher Self to guide you.

*Your Being, not what you do, is your gift to the world. It is the real contribution you make to the world, regardless of your work or expression.*

᭡ ***Write a spontaneous, free flow list of the feelings***

*and qualities of Being you want to live your life from.* Don't edit. Go with your first impulses. Keep your list focused on qualities of feeling, consciousness, and Being from which you want to live your life, not yet addressing what you want to do. If your creative style is more visual, you may begin this experience by creating a collage or a drawing of you embodying your ideal Being qualities, then listing your Being qualities.

- *Read your list out loud to yourself. Notice what sings for you.* If you've created this visually, say, "I see here a man/woman who is living life as . . ." and describe what you've drawn or collaged.

- *Circle the most important qualities* that have the greatest power, feeling, and passion for you.

- *Now turn these into a two- to three-sentence statement of your Vision for Being.* Be playful and spontaneous. Throw out perfection. Let it flow from within you. Whatever you write is perfect for you.

- *Use positive language. Eliminate negatives that push against a state of Being that you don't want.* If you use negatives, you are reminding yourself of what you don't want. Your subconscious mind hears the negative words and phrases you use, and programs them into your state of consciousness.

> *Yes: I, Judith, am a creative, empowered woman leading a life of peace and joy in all I do. I love myself and live my life with zest.*

*What you envision, you start to become with each thought.*

*I hear and I forget.
I see and I remember.
I do and I understand.*

⇒ CHINESE PROVERB

*No: I, Judith, no longer have negative, self-defeating thoughts about myself. I release all self-rejection. I stop judging myself today.*

∾ **State your Being Vision in the present tense.**
Again, your subconscious mind takes your mental and verbal messages about yourself literally. "I will . . ." is interpreted by your subconscious mind as, "I'm not there now. Maybe someday I'll get there . . . ." But someday is always in the future, and your mind responds to this message as "I'm not there yet." State your vision as occurring right now, in the eternal now. You are practicing shifting your state by aligning your thoughts, feelings, and energy to your Being Vision, your highest Self.

∾ **Use "I," your name, and gender to personalize your Being Vision.** "I, Patrick, am a man who is . . . ."
"I, Sophia, am a woman who is . . . ."

Using your name, "I," and gender makes your statement deeply felt, personal, and powerful when you say it to yourself. You own it. This is you. You use your name and gender because your mind identifies with these, so the statement becomes powerful and personal. You connect the words to yourself in a strong manner that brings it home to you.

*I am the light of the world.*

⇒⋆ LESSON FROM
*A Course in Miracles*

## "I Am" Statements of Being

**Your "I am" is the universal Spirit living in you that opens every door and brings positive possibilities to your attention.** Whenever you make an "I am" statement, you are declaring what you believe to be so about yourself. Your word has great power. Our words create our thoughts and feelings, which then lead to what we do and how we live. Be aware of how you limit yourself in negative "I am" statements. Elevate negative statements to positive ones that express the higher truth of your Being.

*"I am connected to the great Source guiding my life."*

What you say you feel, and what you say you are, you become. "I am tired" produces tiredness. "I am frustrated" produces frustration, a feeling that things are not aligned and flowing well for you, which then brings more misaligned events into your experience. "I am in peace" produces a state of peace in you. "I am unconditional love" brings forth your unconditional love, spreading light and positive energy to the world. "I am connected to the great Source guiding my life" potently connects you to your Source. "I am the Divine presence governing all things with positivity and productivity" amplifies the highest potential for great outcomes in all situations you are in.

To me, working this way, metaphysically with "I am" statements, is a blend of being human and real—being allowed to just be crabby or tired and complain about it for a bit if I need to, but not getting stuck there. Be human, with humor, then reach for a higher thought and positive "I am" or Being Vision statement that realigns you back into your Higher Self.

*You, not your current circumstances, are in charge of your state of Being.*

You, not your current circumstances, are in charge of your state of Being. Take charge by practicing positive "I am" statements of Being. Practice weeding out of your speech and thoughts "I am" statements that declare what you do not wish to come true or to strengthen. I have a practice: when I find myself saying, "I am tired of . . .," or "I am sick of . . .," I know on some level that I am declaring things I do not really want to be living from. Instead I practice trying to interrupt myself and changing my language to, "I am *complete* with . . .," "I am

*ready to move on* from . . . ," "I am *finding a solution* to . . . ," "I
love learning how to . . . ."

Because I am just a human being on the path, I sometimes complain, whine, and judge like everyone else. But I
see how doing so brings my vibrational state down, and I
try to catch myself as soon as I can, realigning my speech
and thoughts back to the truth of who I am.

The ego loves the shallow satisfaction of criticizing
others and making victimized statements. While we all
need to feel the passing emotions going through us and
honor them as what's in the room right now, without denial
or suppression, don't fall into saying, "This is who I am."
Acknowledge your passing emotions, but don't invite them
to take up residence and define who you are.

You are the light of the world. Who you truly are is
a great Being, connected at the Source to the vast cosmic
energy that feeds and nourishes and grows everything on
the earth. Next time you feel tired, practice taking deep
breaths and declaring how well you are, how well you feel,
and how your health is the expression of the one great
Mind and Being. It may feel phony in the beginning,
because most of us tend to identify with our immediate
experiences as real, but you will be surprised how quickly
your energy shifts as you stand in "I am" statements of
your higher truth, the truth that is you.

Many people put the reins of their moment in the
hands of their immediate symptoms and say, "Ok, you take
over and tell me how to be." Instead, take charge! Choose
your Higher Self, repeat your Being Vision, speak with
passionately felt, positive "I am" statements, and watch
your state and energy shift.

*Who you truly are
is a great Being,
connected at the
Source to the vast
cosmic energy that
feeds and nourishes
and grows
everything on the
earth.*

# Practicing Being

Now bring your Being Vision alive by practicing it until it becomes natural and part of you, a way of thinking about you and your life. Here are helpful ways to practice living from your Being Vision.

## Beautiful Mornings: Your Spiritual Practice

I grew up in a metaphysical household where my mother, a full-time executive secretary raising two daughters alone, rose early, made tea and toast, and sat on the living room couch in silence, sipping her tea, and studying her Christian Science spiritual textbooks, before sinking into deep prayer. I can see her in my mind's eye in her pink satin, quilted robe, eyes closed, tea and toast before her, her finger on her lips as she repeated her statements of spiritual Being to herself. She was scripting her day for the highest good and aligning herself to God, while also holding my sister and me in her prayers. My sister Betsy and I got ready for school while Mom did her "morning work."

And now, I start most of my days the same way, no matter where I am, travelling, vacationing, or at home, with

*For those leaning on the sustaining Infinite, today is big with blessings.*

≥❋ MARY BAKER EDDY

tea and toast and quiet meditation. When I travel, whether teaching or vacationing, I take a lightweight teapot and toaster, and make my own toast and tea in my room, creating a quiet, sacred space for myself before entering the day outside. I bring a mug and a tea towel from home to set up a cozy space, a magical sanctuary where I can rest and sink in to start my day. At home or on the road, this simple practice has brought me through many challenging times and given me peace and help.

If you don't already meditate, start tomorrow morning. Don't wait until you have an overwhelming health or emotional crisis, when attuning is harder, to give yourself the gift of a beautiful spiritual practice. Your meditation can be brief if your life is busy: give yourself at least ten to fifteen minutes of peaceful stillness, without external activities, to align yourself with your Highest Self, to remember your Being Vision, and to breathe and connect with God within you. In Phase 1, I give instructions for meditation and offer ways to wrangle with the chatty mind popping in with the agendas of the small self.

When you sink into your quiet space, repeat your Being Vision. Let it guide your day moving forward.

## Practices for Deepening Being

Here are further helpful practices for living from your Being Vision.

*Every blade of grass has its angel that bends over it and whispers, "Grow, grow."*

≈✳ THE TALMUD

〜 *Repeat your Being Vision to yourself when you awaken in the morning.* Forge your day in this powerful way. Feel the energy of this vision on a cellular level as you stretch awake and enter another day of your life on Planet Earth. Let gratitude for the good in your life fill your heart on awakening. Live from your Highest Self, and let your Being Vision take you there. Affirm only positive outcomes from everything currently taking place in your life.

﹏ *Live this day of your life from your Being Vision.* See the day unfolding in front of you as a natural, beautiful expression of your Being Vision, flowing out into manifested forms, doing, interacting, and taking action. You don't have to stand on the mountain top with scrolls from the Divine to have an experience of living from your Being Vision. You still go to work, feed your children and drive them to school, pay your bills, and grocery shop, but from an entirely new frame of mind: from your Being Vision. Miracles occur in life's normal moments when you shift your consciousness through deliberately choosing to remember and practice knowing who you really are: your Being Vision.

﹏ *Make your Being Vision a mantra, your personal prayer. Mentally repeat it many times in your day, letting it fill you with well being and peace.* Repeat it to yourself when you find yourself feeling resentful, worried, or resistant to what is occurring around you. You cannot control all outer circumstances, but you have the power of great creative direction of your thoughts and state of Being. You are in charge of your thoughts and, therefore, your consciousness.

∽ ***Post it where you'll see and remember it.*** Make a sign with your Being Vision for your bathroom mirror, your car dashboard, or over your desk. Each time you see your Being Vision, remember what really matters to you in your life.

∽ ***When making both big decisions and daily life choices, think of your Being Vision.*** Then ask yourself, "If I am living from my Being Vision, what choice do I make about this?" This is as simple as who you have lunch with today, or as big as pursuing new work or new relationships, taking a major trip, or moving to a new locale. Attuning to your Being Vision becomes a golden ruler to measure each choice in terms of your highest vision for yourself.

∽ ***Embody It.*** If you love to walk, walk it. If you dance, dance it. If you swim, swim it. Think of your Being Vision while breathing and moving in any way at all, including walking down a hall or strolling to the grocery store. Move it into your cellular knowing, so that it becomes part of you. Move and stand, walk and embody yourself as the man or woman who lives from this state of Being.

∽ ***Be Self-ish:*** Choose your day's activities to support your Being Vision, as well as the Doing you'll create in Phase 4. When invitations and opportunities arise, take time to consider your being and purpose, and choose what's most aligned.

## Being versus Planning

*There is a fresh new way that things can take shape and be manifested through us when we get out of the way and, just for a time, give up planning everything and practice Being.* Midway through writing *Navigating Change*, I was meditating on our acequia deck in Santa Fe, the wooden deck my husband and I built over the running water that flows through New Mexico's ancient irrigation channels several months of the year. It was time for my vision check-in with my life. I loved sitting there getting ready to revision my life, steeped in the magic that happens when we write down our life goals and Being Visions and get in touch with the limitless dreams of our lives perking inside us. I was perched on a patio chair with my journal and inspirational books *du jour*, sipping Irish Breakfast tea to the background music of the acequia waters rolling underneath the deck.

As a teacher of vision and metaphysics, I try to revisit my own vision at least twice a year for a check-in; kind of a psychic tune-up to keep myself and my actions and thoughts aligned to my highest calling, and make sure I'm not galloping off down some path—a friendship or work opportunity or plan—that is not aligned to my greatest good. These vision check-ins keep me on track with my most important values, and insure that my outer decisions and choices are serving my Being, my highest good.

This book was more than halfway done, and I was ready to charge ahead in a big push to complete it. In meditation, I called on Spirit and Higher Self and asked: "What do you want me to do now?" These inner dialogues often bring in wisdom greater than that of my limited ego-mind, and I get great gifts from asking and then paying attention to what spontaneously pops in.

*Give up planning, and the world will be a thousand times better.*

⇒✷ LAO TZU,
*Tao Te Ching*

*When we let Spirit lead us*

*It is impossible to know where we are being led.*

*All we know, all we can believe, all we can hope,*

*Is that we are going home;*

*That wherever Spirit takes us*

*Is where we live.*

≋ ALICE WALKER

Today's answer, however, truly astonished me. "Give up planning," I heard from my own inner guidance. *Give up planning?* Yes. That was the message coming through, absolutely.

Sometimes we ask for guidance, but don't like what we hear because it threatens our modus operandi. But often that out-of-the-blue answer that rocks our universe IS the greatest, wisest response, and it's our job to heed it.

I began to practice giving up planning. I found that I still wrote my book, and kept my client appointments, and grocery shopped. The horses and cats got fed and so did I. But these actions began to take place from a very different vantage point. I was learning to respond to what was happening right here, right now. I have an appointment to see a client? I dress and show up, I read the file notes, I tune in; but give up planning. This creates a fresh openness, freed of my own mental concepts about what to do in a situation, which can actually inhibit a greater intelligence from coming through.

I began to practice this in finishing this book. Suddenly, the writing flowed in a new way that I hadn't found before. I was letting Spirit help me write, instead of doing it all myself.

## Getting Out of Our Own Way: Being Led by Spirit

It is extraordinary what happens through us when we get out of our own way and let Spirit run the show. After morning meditation, I lit a candle, and called on Spirit to write, then did my best to "give up planning" and step out of the way. It was a revolutionary way of writing and working for me, one that challenged all my control issues and threw my lengthy book outlines out the window.

I found that what came through was automatically more organized and coherent, with more soulfulness of content, than many earlier efforts that had hit the wastebasket. Time flew, and the unplanned book-writing of several hours had a structure and flow beyond anything I could do with my ego-mind in a few weeks of struggling. The anxieties that all creative people must contend with were suspended for a time by this simple practice. If "I" am not writing, then "I" can let go of the results. A wisdom surpassing that of my conscious mind can come through.

It's not enough to give up planning and sit around waiting for inspiration to strike while we light candles and chant Om. We need a power cord that hooks us up with our Higher Power. Our power cords are our spiritual practices, whatever they are. Meditation, prayer, or any spiritual practices that connect us to our own Higher Powers provide a different kind of internal planning or guidance that tells us how to move forward. In our empty, receptive moments, we clear our decks to see life's potentials and opportunities showing up in fresh new ways.

Before we paint on our own life canvases, those canvases need to be blank. The answers we access when our busy minds "give up planning" for a time may astound us with their lucidity and clarity. Just for a short time, give up planning, practice Being supported by your Being Vision, connect to your own Higher Power, and see what happens next.

# SECTION 5

# Coming Home to Ourselves:
# New Being, New Life

### Freeing the Tiger:
### Rebecca Recovers Her True Self

Rebecca called me several years ago for a three-day Personal Intensive Retreat in my Santa Fe studio. She shared feelings of low self-esteem, her reliance on antidepressants and drugs to sleep, and the persistent feeling that something was out of whack in her life. She described times of emotionally falling apart and feeling that she was a big mess. But I saw something different inside of the sweet, shaky woman with long strawberry-blonde hair sitting before me. I saw a strong, bright woman, full of vigor and intelligence and spunk, just waiting to be recognized and invited into the room.

"I've had nightmares about a tiger coming after me for years," she said. "I'm running terrified, the tiger on my heels. The tiger chases me into my house, where I hide inside a cabinet, afraid to come out."

"What do tigers mean to you?" I asked.

"Power, danger. Excitement. Bigness. They're so alive, but also scary," Rebecca said. Her dream revealed her fear of her own power and bigness of Self.

"Sometimes figures in dreams are important soul friends wanting to help us grow, even if they feel terrifying. Let's chat with this tiger and see what he has to say," I invited her. "What might your tiger say if you turned around and met him?"

"Well, he'd say, 'It's about time we met. I have been chasing you because I want to know you. Why do you run from me? I only seem dangerous because you won't let me in. I'm right in your own house. Come out of the cabinet you're hiding in"—I saw the cabinet as possibly symbolizing Rebecca's overweight body—"and let me see you. I won't bite you.'"

"Rebecca, let's reconsider the possibility that the tiger is a friend who wishes you well, who is trying to meet you and help you. Maybe these dreams are a way for the tiger within you to get your attention and ask for connection. I wonder what might happen if you greet him and see what gifts he has for you?"

Rebecca thought. "Well, the gift of my own power. My feisty self. I don't feel very feisty or powerful," she admitted. "And my husband tells me what a mess I am all the time, how my cooking isn't very good, and I don't handle business calls well. But he's really a great man," she rushed to say. Rebecca had a husband who was not interested in having a tigress in the house and, consciously or unconsciously, minimized her by putting her expression and creativity down at every turn. She was colluding by collapsing and taking on the role of the self-doubting woman, making herself the sole problem. "Plus I am clinically depressed. I saw a psychiatrist and he diagnosed me. I have to take anti-depressants every day."

It was time to end our first retreat session. "Enjoy your break. Take your tiger along with you. He might enjoy a little outing." She laughed. "You might like going to the Tesuque Flea Market to wander and find treasures."

The next morning, Rebecca showed up for her retreat with a big smile. "Look what I found at the flea market!" she crowed, unfurling a big hand-woven rug. "I just walked into this booth, and there it was—my tiger!" She held up a beautiful Tibetan rug with a bold tiger in the center. I noticed the tiger was now "my tiger" to her, and marveled again at the striking symmetry of the universe, always matching what's inside of us with the outside symbols. "I can't wait to take this rug home and hang it up in my home office!" Now she was on the road back to owning herself.

A couple of months later, we were on the phone in a follow-up session. We had done much deep work, and I never heard her speak about feeling sad or depressed. She again referred to her clinical diagnosis. "Well, I'm just a depressed person."

"Rebecca, I'm not sure about that. There certainly is such a thing as clinical depression, but you and I have spent hours in sessions now, and I hear a lot of energy, anger, joy, fear, excitement—but have never once heard you say that you feel depressed."

This was met with a long silence. But in our next session, Rebecca announced, "I thought about what you said, and you're right. I'm not depressed! I threw away my antidepressants and I feel great! I am also not taking drugs to sleep anymore. I have a little insomnia, but I'm using vitamins and herbs to help."

*Within every woman is a wild and natural creature, a powerful force, filled with good instincts, passionate creativity and ageless knowing. Her name is: Wild Woman.*

≈❋ CLARISSA PINKOLA ESTES, *Women Who Run With the Wolves*

Rebecca eventually divorced her denigrating husband who didn't wish to be married to a powerhouse Scottish-American woman with a tiger in her office. She began to run again and work out at a gym with a trainer. She lost fifty pounds the first year, then eighty-five, and now has lost one hundred pounds and kept them off for years. She took up long-distance cycling. She became an active volunteer in races and cycling events to raise money for a charity helping those with M.S., making new friends everywhere she went.

She took a cruise, something her husband had always kept her from doing, although she made a six-figure income on her own. She contacted old friends who were delighted to have her merry spirit back in their lives. She did extraordinary work at her IT company and was promoted to a global directorship position. She sold the big house she and her husband had owned and bought a charming, smaller one with a garden she loves. I sent her a candle lantern as a housewarming gift, with an electric candle that turns on at dusk each day, a reminder of the light within her always present. We have kept in touch with occasional sessions as she needs them over the years.

We spoke recently. Once a bankrupt, insecure young woman leaning on her take-charge husband, last week Rebecca graduated from a distinguished university with a degree in leadership, won while working a demanding, fulltime job, negotiating a divorce, buying a house, navigating the loss of a beloved parent, and creating her new life.

I mentioned the old tiger dreams of long ago. "Christine, do you know that from the minute I bought that tiger rug and hung it up in my home, I have not had one more dream about tigers?"

"Your tiger is out! And she is you in all her glory, Rebecca. This is what happens when we face and integrate the parts of ourselves calling for connection and life. You are an amazing woman! Good work!"

## Coming Out: Gretchen's Journey of Change

*There is only one life you can call your own And a thousand others you can call by any name you want.*

≋✴ DAVID WHYTE, "All the True Vows"

***Esprit is the spirit of aliveness and passion to live the life for which we are born.*** My client Gretchen embodies esprit, and her tale of coming out as a lesbian later in life shows the way to make huge changes with our arms around all of it: Being first, then doing; human and spiritual embracing.

Gretchen's last name is Courage, and that defines her. Her story is a modern heroine's journey of a woman navigating a major life change with zest. I once commented to her, "You do everything with total enthusiasm. You even suffer enthusiastically!"

Gretchen left a forty-year marriage to come out as a lesbian, moving to Northampton, Massachusetts, a stronghold of gay and lesbian community. Before her bold outer move, she spent decades exploring the complex terrain of being bisexual, loving her traditional heterosexual family life, her affection for her husband, and enjoyment of her home, gardens, and Episcopal church community. She was open with her husband about her bisexuality and her attractions to women, and they ongoingly explored how to mesh their marriage with her bisexuality. At one point, I said to Gretchen, "Someday you will have to make a choice: to let go of your life as a straight married woman, or to let go of pursuing relationships with women. The split is too difficult for you to carry."

After years of exploring her own change terrain, Gretchen made the bold decision to step fully into her life as a lesbian, turning her life upside down. At sixty-one she came out and moved to Northampton. I was privileged to witness and facilitate her inner work throughout her passage.

Her Christmas letter that year to friends, sharing the inner workings of her transition, exemplifies a woman who is working all four phases of change: integrating her endings with feeling and authenticity; facing the Mystery times of chaos and confusion; discovering a new Being Vision in peace and reflection, in nature, and spiritual practices; and, finally, meshing her inner shifts with artistic, athletic, and musical activities—a Doing Vision she has created that nourishes her. Since writing this letter, Gretchen met and married a great woman and recreated her career to become a Montessori consultant. I share excerpts from her letter here with her permission.

*Dear Family and Friends,*

*My Christmas card takes a different form this year, just as my life does. Instead of a photograph of a smiling family of four, I offer a reflection on my life at this moment of transition. After forty years, Richard and I are ending our marriage. We are committed to a respectful and amicable relationship as we enter this new stage on our life journeys. I will always cherish my marriage to Richard and our vibrant and caring children, whom we continue to co-parent with complete love and devotion. I cherish my family.*

*Holding sadness and gratitude together in the same heart makes it feel like breaking sometimes, but it is the real and authentic life that offers the fullness that I want. I am honored to have the name Courage and always do my utmost to live up to it. I invoke courage as I step into unknown territory. "What is really happening here?" accompanies me like a companion with whom I have learned to travel well.*

*The adventures on the inside as I navigate these profound life changes are reflected in the adventures on the outside. In nature, in women's hikes, in the forest, I find both revitalizing energy and peaceful comfort in the natural world. In the words of Wendell Berry, "I come into the presence of still water . . . for a time I rest in the grace of the world, and am free."*

*I am living in a beautiful studio in Northampton in the home of dear friends. My favorite chaise lounge now looks out on a different view. I sit there each morning before dawn, write in my journal, meditate, and read poetry. This is my home now; this is where my family and friends visit. My "stuff" is here, and a few plants from the garden I created in my marriage have made the move with me. Wilbur, my cat, is here for purring support.*

*I am becoming a serious student of yoga and meditation. When fear, grief, or confusion are, in Rumi's words, "visiting the guest house," I find that getting my body in alignment leads to emotional alignment as well. We laugh a lot in yoga class and laughter lines things up better than anything else I know.*

*Drumming is my passion and I am a member of Off-beat, a women's percussion ensemble. Oh yes, I have my job too, a mentor in the Montessori public schools, challenging and rewarding work. I am grateful to spend my days with children and do work that I love.*

*I am grateful for my friends; I am filled by your presence in my life. You include me in comforting and familiar rituals, dinner around the table, snuggling on the sofa, crying and laughing together, cooking together, boogieing at lesbian dances, attending workshops and retreats, running and hiking. All this familiarity is very grounding and appreciated by the New Me as I come out, and at the same time, come more fully into myself . . . . I dig deep within as we enter the winter months.*

    *With Love and Appreciation of this one life,*
      *Gretchen*

## Kimba's Story: The Snake Sheds Its Skin

I met Kimba at the opening night of my workshop "Lifewalk: The Hero's Journey and the Spiritual Quest" at Rowe Camp and Conference Center, a retreat center of old farmhouses, log cabins, and barns located in the pre-revolutionary forests of Rowe, Massachusetts. The workshop was situated in the living room of an eighty-year-old farmhouse with plump, faded couches, tea brewing in the snack corner, candles in the windowsills, and Celtic music filling the room. Arriving guests stomped snow off their boots, threw coats on an old armchair, and greeted one another in nervous anticipation.

    We formed a standing circle, holding hands. I invited the group to meet each other soul to soul through music and eye contact. My assistant, Sonya, turned up a piece of music by Peter Kater and Carlos Nakai, and ancient Native American chanting, shamanic flutes, and piano filled our space. The air felt electric with possibilities. We stepped together out of our modus operandi into the

> *The wound is the place where the light enters you.*
>
> ⇒✳ RUMI

inviting mystery of the weekend. A fresh new space for being alive had been opened up.

In this moment, the workshop room door opened. In walked Kimba, a redheaded woman in her forties with thick glasses, engulfed in a fluorescent-orange down jacket that matched her choppy carrot hair. Her eyes were wide with fear, her face frozen, defended in advance against us. She seemed to be asking, "Am I safe here? Is it okay to enter? Will you receive me?" I reached out and welcomed her, pulling her into the circle beside me as I squeezed her hand. I wanted our newborn group field to communicate to her, "We welcome you. You're safe here. You belong with us. Step out of the night cold and into our circle."

The next day beamed icy bright as we dove into our Lifewalk morning activities, journaling, painting self-portraits of our limitless selves, sharing in small groups, doing wild boogieing and scarfing up dark chocolate on breaks to ground all the intense inner work. As we moved through the morning, estranged pieces of ourselves came home for healing. At one point I saw Kimba remove her big coat and let her million-watt smile shine. She relaxed into the circle of other caring, authentic people sharing their own trials and challenges. She was finding tribe.

Lunch, naps, and rest time passed. The afternoon sun broke through winter's grey-sky blanket. We were now on a quest to face fears and find symbols of power, a phase of the hero's journey. We hiked into the forest, our guardians the towering blue-green firs, our guides the two hundred fifty-year-old stone walls. Bundled in down and fleece, the group scattered along a snowy riverbed talking to stones. Each poured personal fears into her chosen rock, preparing to ritually release it into the running water. I felt a tap on my shoulder.

Kimba stood gazing at me, frozen in place like a deer in the headlights. Behind the large, thick glasses, her blue eyes were wide with terror.

"I need help. I'm going to have a panic attack, Christine. I'm terrified of snakes. I'm petrified a snake will come along."

"What do snakes mean to you?"

"When I was growing up, my brother abused me with cruel tricks. Once on a family camping trip, he filled my sleeping bag with live snakes and waited for me to crawl into it, then laughed hysterically when I freaked out. I've been terrified of snakes ever since."

I felt my own body shudder with the horror of her experience. I wrapped my arms around her shaking shoulders, holding her close like a protective mama bear. She melted into the hug, pulled out of past trauma in the warmth of simple human touch.

"Breathe with me, Kimba. Let's breathe together. Fear and breath cannot coexist. All is well right here and now. You are safe. There are no snakes here in this moment."

Her sobs soaked my fleece jacket. We stood together until she felt calm again. Then Sonya took her hand and walked her back to the candlelit warmth of our workshop space as the group finished their rituals.

When we returned, Kimba was shaking, but this time with excitement.

"I found a snake skin!" she announced to the group. "Lying right on the road! When Sonya left me here to return to you guys, I went back outside on my own. I wanted to face my fears. I found a snake skin! I'm finished with my fear. It's over! I'm free!"

The group laughed and cheered and said in unison our group mantra, "We see you!" Her big eyes danced. She had

*Our traumas and past suffering do not define us. We define us.*

broken through an old trauma, and had done it on her own, with just a little help from our workshop tribe.

Two years later, I received a Shutterfly book she'd created titled, "Celebrating Me." The book shared her creation of a baptism for her new self, an immersion in a New England lake witnessed by three close friends, two of whom she'd met in her Rowe workshop. Photographs showed her wading into the icy September water as she released the old Kimba. Other photos showed her circle of friends welcoming her back with warm blankets, hugs, and hot coffee. She photographed the event, created the book, and sent it to her friends.

I cried when I saw myself in her acknowledgements as one who had helped "call her forth" into her new, joyful life. Her book had arrived at a time when I was struggling with my own value as a teacher. The gift went full circle, seeing and being seen, helping and being helped. Kimba had arrived in her new life and was now shining her light to everyone around her, including me.

Our traumas and past suffering do not define us. We define us. We choose our rituals, our tribes, and our moments of power. We face our fears and receive stunning symbols declaring our worth and freedom. Our determination to grow unlocks the doors to our liberation. Behind the door of fear, we discover who we are in truth: strong, loved, safe, and able to give and receive.

## Giving Up Practicing the Being Vision

**When you practice your Being Vision with gratitude and positive energy, it eventually becomes your default position.** It assumes you. Our normal human insecurities, worries, and fears still show up—and on some days, they seem to run the show of our lives—but now you see them as opportunities to remember who you truly are and come home to Being. Reaching for your higher thoughts, your Being Vision, becomes natural. And when that happens you can give up practicing your Being Vision and just *be*.

Once you've gotten it, you can let it go. Like all spiritual and inner practices, it is just a tool to bring you into living more in the moment, less in future plans; more in love and less in fear. It's a marvelous training method to invite your mind to inhabit the state of Being you want to live from, and make that state a beautiful mental habit. Like this book, the Being Vision is a stepping stone on the path of your life.

If you have done the processes described here, you are ready to create your outer expression. You'll create it in Phase 4, increasingly living from your Source and remembering that your joy is right here in the moment, not in some future created form.

*Just take what you need and leave the rest.*

⇒ THE BAND

*From the place of being rooted in*
*your values for Being, you will be a magnificent*
*channel and creator of what is to*
*come next in your life.*

*You are ready for*
*Phase 4 of Navigating Change:*
*"Visionary Beginnings: Creating from the Source."*
*Read on!*

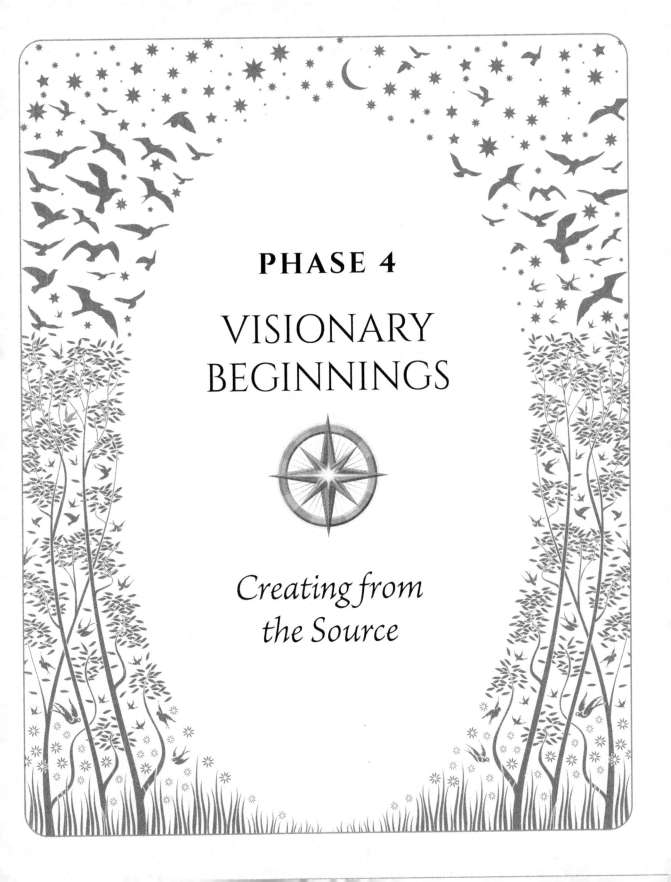

# PHASE 4

## VISIONARY BEGINNINGS

*Creating from the Source*

# PHASE 4

*හ*

# Visionary Beginnings:
# Creating from the Source

When you've consciously gone through your journey of change, ended well, drawn wisdom and trust from the Mystery, and found your new Being, you arrive at the day when you feel called to begin a new vision or expression in your life. You're in Phase 4 ~ Visionary Beginnings. The boxes titled **ॐ** *Inspired Practice* offer you experiential exercises for applying these teachings to begin creating and living your life vision.

As you tap into your vision and find faith and confidence to live it, magical synchronicities, new possibilities, and surprising connections start appearing, as if they were just waiting to show up all this time. Phase 4 explains just how this extraordinary metaphysical process occurs and how you can use this knowledge to bring your visions into reality.

*Follow your intuition of where your joy is.*

*You will be helped by hidden forces when you determine to follow your bliss, and do it with joy and a positive, expectant attitude.*

*You put yourself on a track that has been there waiting for you all along, and the life you are living becomes the life you are supposed to be living.*

*≈ JOSEPH CAMPBELL*

Phase 4 is divided into four sections, guiding you in creating and manifesting what you wish to express next in your life. The sections are:

# The Tao of Physics, Metaphysics, and Your Life

## The Field Where We Live

There is an entirely new way to find and live your visionary new beginnings in your life, one that is full of ease, joy, and peace. Before you try to create a new vision for your life, take time to understand where you live, here in this field of consciousness, and how all things actually manifest, or come into form. Phase 4, Visionary Beginnings, starts at the beginning, by understanding the field where you live, then applies this wisdom to creating new beginnings in your life.

Grounding yourself into a larger understanding of who you are and how things occur helps you travel forward from an entirely new understanding of how things come into creation from the Source. You will learn how to transcend rushing around, competing, and striving to get your dreams and visions accomplished in the outer world. You'll be moving forward with greater ease and joy than from your old ways of making things happen in your life.

*The most beautiful thing we can experience is the mysterious. It is the source of all true art and science.*

≈ ALBERT EINSTEIN

*Matter is Spirit moving slowly enough to be seen.*

≋✶ TEILHARD DE
CHARDIN

You are an infinite, creative being, because you are part of God. You are constantly connected to your Source, or Spirit, which is always helping you, supporting you, and guiding you. You are limitless in your capacity to heal, express, and create in your life when you become aware of this deep truth and begin to live life attuned to your connection to Source. When you make this shift in awareness, you have the ability to create your life from an entirely new place. You realize that, regardless of how things appear around you, you are never powerless, nor are you ever limited or constricted by presenting circumstances or others' choices and decisions.

Ancient mystical paths have told us that we are all part of God, part of All that is. In our time, the revolutionary findings of quantum physics have given new support to the deep truths of many ancient mystical teachings. The findings of quantum physicists have shaken up and transformed our understanding of what life consists of, who we are, who others are, and how things come into being. They are so important that I want to begin this phase by sharing some extraordinary highlights from them.

The universe is a dynamic web of interconnection, and all that appears to us as forms exists according to our perceptions of it. We appear to be individual human beings living separate lives, but, in truth, we are all profoundly, intrinsically interconnected, all one Spirit. On a global level, the collective consciousness of the world, including ours, shapes the forms we see according to what we believe and carry in our thoughts and Being. As more of us awaken, change, and evolve, the outer world shifts to mirror the new consciousness being held by growing numbers of people. This book is about personal change and your personal life journey, so we'll focus on how these teachings translate into your visionary new beginnings.

*What we call life is an optical illusion of consciousness.*

≋✶ ALBERT EINSTEIN

How do we know this is true? Quantum physicists wanted to understand what matter consists of, to discover what the world of form is actually constructed of. In examining matter down to the tiniest particles—from molecules to atoms, from atoms to protons, electrons, and neutrons, down to quarks—ultimately they found that at the source of all matter, *nothing exists but pure energy*, vibrating at different rates, and appearing to us as solid objects. This is so foreign to our habituated way of thinking about the world and our lives that we might pause and consider that who we are, and how we manifest the forms in our lives, is not as we have thought. By understanding these profound truths of how things in our lives come into being as an alignment of our thoughts, perceptions and expectations, we are empowered in creating our new visions for our lives.

## The Power of Perception: We Find What We Are Seeking

*What force is shaping the pure energy of the quantum field into forms we recognize, including the shapes of our own lives?* Quantum scientists wanted to know why the field of pure, vibrating energy appears to us as particular forms. In a finding titled, "The Observer Effect," quantum researchers further studied matter, each seeking certain data or results. Over time, they began to notice a startling phenomenon: the unique data each researcher was looking for seemed to be showing up on the slide. Quantum physicists deduced that the consciousness, or focused expectations and thoughts, that is being directed at the field is actually influencing what is found.

As the creators of our lives, we are constantly expanding, limiting, or influencing our possibilities, creatively,

*I am large; I contain multitudes.*

≈ WALT WHITMAN

*Every man's world picture is always a construct of his mind and has no other existence.*

≈ ERWIN SCHRÖDINGER

relationally, professionally, and personally, to align to what we believe to be true. Take a moment and consider the great impact of this knowledge in your life. What you are observing as the world around you, including the content of your own life, is continually, subtly influenced by the consciousness, the thoughts, and the feelings you have regarding it. What you are expecting to find in others and in life is continually shaping the possibilities of what comes to you.

You are directing your life every day according to your thoughts, your consciousness, your state of Being, and your expectations. This is going on all the time whether you believe it or not, and whether you are aware of the process or not. Your thoughts are constantly materializing as your experiences of the outer world. You see in yourself, in others, and in life what you expect to see. There's no there, there—just what you expect to find and project outward from your perceptions and thoughts. As a piece of God, an expression of the one Spirit, you are that powerful, and that limitless.

*The objective world rises from the mind itself.*

❀ The Buddha

## Thought, Intention, and Vibration: The Palette from Which You Paint Your Life

**You are an artist, and your life is your outward creation.** It's the visible expression of all of the thoughts, intentions, and vision you have held up to this moment, now showing up as what you see. You have a palette of colors with which you are always painting your life: a rainbow of possible thoughts, vibrations, intentions, and expectations are there to choose from. The moment you choose different colors, select different thoughts, and live from a different level of Being and vision, your life changes.

We do not attract what we want, we attract what we *are*. Being comes first, and our resulting thoughts, feelings, and vibrational states follow. This palette composed of our Being, thoughts, expectations, and deeply held feelings becomes the material with which we are painting our lives, every day. How we move forward on our paths through life is powerfully determined by the states of Being we hold, and the resulting positive or negative thoughts and beliefs we each have about what's possible.

Hold a clear Being Vision of the kind of person you wish to be, and then do what you can to become that person, connected to your Source, your Higher Self. Next, write down your vision for your new beginning, whatever you are wishing to bring into your life. When you do this, opportunities come flowing in as you are truly ready. The details of your life align in beautiful ways that expand and support you.

This does not mean you'll never be disappointed, not get what you thought you wanted, suffer, be ill, or endure challenges, as these are part of your soul curriculum, described in Phase 1. Our soul curriculum is always unfolding through situations that invite us to go deeper, become wiser, live from our truths, and move forward guided by our Source, Spirit, or Higher Self. What we perceive as things not working out according to what we thought would be best for us are often the greatest gifts for our growth and well-being, saving us from situations that would not have truly served us, or pointing us forward in new, more positive directions.

What you envision with greatest consistency, feeling, and expectation is what shows up. When you know you are connected to the Source of All that is, and when you remember how things are actually manifesting, or coming into form, all the time, you can utilize this ancient wisdom

*Seek ye first the kingdom of God, and all these things will be added unto you.*

— CHRIST

*We do not attract what we want, we attract what we are.*

to attune to the greatest blessing and possibility for your own life and for all engaged in any situation you enter. You become a blessing to the world just through your presence.

As you create visionary new beginnings in your life, you affirm that your greatest fulfillment and good are now expressing themselves through every person and situation. When difficulties arise, embrace them as opportunities to remember who you really are, and who others are also, and invite in great solutions and opportunities. Put Being first, then the universe matches your positive energy with a resonant response.

When you clearly know the right next action for you, you follow that guidance. When your actions in life stem from your connection with your Source, which is the same as your Higher Self, then your outward life changes, often in astonishing ways. Extraordinary synchronicities begin to occur, and things unfold that you never could have imagined. You are moving from new ground, supported in living a life that is a gift to you and to everyone you encounter.

## Our World Reflects Our State of Being

*We are continually restructuring our world according to the changes of our thoughts and presence, or our state of Being.* Our Being carries an energy field, or vibration, that influences and determines the outcome of everything we do and our experience of everyone we encounter. To know this is to stand in your spiritual power and mastery and know you are never the victim of circumstances or outer events. You are the director of the movie of your life. And you can change it at any moment by the state of Being you choose to live from and the thoughts, expectations, intentions, and presence you bring to each day.

*Things are not the way they are. They are the way we are.*

≈ THE TALMUD

This is why I've emphasized the importance of a spiritual or meditative practice in this book, one that you love doing. We can access miracles in our lives when we begin each day by dropping deeply into our center of Being, and letting go of struggling so that the voice of our Source and Higher Self can be heard. Then our entire day flows differently. How we live our days becomes our weeks, and our weeks become our lives. It all begins right now, right here, not with a mental to-do list that reiterates what you used to do and how you used to create things in your life, but through living from your higher state of Being, connected to God, or the Source of All that is. Then right action follows. What we then create or do becomes the outward expression of our Being, and our doing always reflects our states of Being.

We need to remember and know how things actually come into form before beginning any new visionary expression in our lives, so we are moving from a higher truth of who we are and how we are one with that world through which we seek to express ourselves. I find that this deep truth of how everything exists liberates me when I become stressed, or go into fear and struggle, and forget who I truly am. When I remember who I am and return home to Being, I find peace and trust in life's unfolding plan for me, and then everything starts to flow again.

This beginning to Phase 4, Visionary Beginnings, has laid the groundwork for all you create next through understanding your Source, the unified field that you exist within. You're now ready to create your vision for the next chapter of your life.

*When you change the way you look at things, what you look at changes.*

≋ WAYNE DYER

# Beautiful Beginnings:
# Creating Your Vision
# for Your Next Expression

*There is a vitality, a life force, an energy, a quickening that is translated through you into action, and because there is only one of you in all of time, this expression is unique.*

*It is not your business to determine how good it is nor how it compares with other expressions. It is your business to keep it yours clearly and directly, to keep the channel open.*

≳ MARTHA GRAHAM

## Wanted: Your Voice in the World

**T**o live our true callings in life, we need to take the *paths that align to what we really love.* My friend Kamini called me years ago from Europe. "I'm entering a Ph.D. program here, and I want to ask your advice. I want to major in psychology and teach and give wonderful workshops, but my father wants me to go into business, so I'll always have something to fall back on. What do you think?"

I remembered her grace while teaching yoga, the fire in her eyes leading dance, the way her classes lit up Kripalu's workshop guests with vitality, love, and joy. "Isn't it interesting how we go to the people for advice who will tell us what we want to hear?" I teased her. "What do you *want* to do with your life?"

"Teach workshops in personal growth and spirituality!"

"What academic path aligns to your vision?"

She laughed, the answer being obvious. "I'm going to get a Ph.D. in psychology," she declared with relief.

"And I will be cheering for you all the way," I responded.

Today, Kamini Desai has touched thousands of people with her inspiring workshops, her books, and her uplifting presence. She found her path with heart by taking time to connect to her true values for Being—her deep spirituality, her love of teaching and helping people, her joy in dance and yoga—instead of making a security-based decision of having something to "fall back on" that was not her true path. Instead, she asked herself what her true calling was—asking me as an older mentor for help in clarifying that—then took the path aligned to her real love. She is a light to all who know her.

## How Does a Vision Manifest?

Here are the steps that lead to a vision becoming actualized in your life.

1. *You have a wish,* which becomes a strong desire for expression in your life.

2. *Your desire deepens, and you form a focused intention for your vision,* with positive, expectant energy. You write this down in clear, powerful language, as guided in the coming pages.

3. *You connect to Spirit, God, or your Higher Self,* accessing inspiration and ideas that supersede those available from your limited ego self.

*Affirm your highest good. Affirmations put your thoughts into words, and words have power.*

≈ NANA VEARY

4. *You clear and open your channels,* so that inspiration and vision can easily move through you. You do this by:

    ~ *Releasing blocking emotions* by feeling and healing them.

    ~ *Raising your energy* through vital, healthy living, deep breathing, life-giving foods, and movement that bring forth your greatest vitality.

    ~ *Meditating or doing a spiritual practice* you love which brings you into the present moment and bypasses constricting fears and limiting thoughts.

5. *You align your thinking, actions, and energy to your vision.* You embody it. You experience the positive, uplifting feelings of this vision as if it were already present in your life.

6. *The universe matches your vision by bringing you opportunities and insights for action.* Note that these arrive in divine timing, which is always just right for your unfoldment and growth, but may be different from the timing your ego or small self would like.

## Creating a New Vision

*It's time to bring your callings and dreams into a Doing Vision, one that expresses who you have become.* The following guidance leads you through the creation of your vision, which is the outer expression of the Being Vision you created in Phase 3.

Creating a new vision for your life is an exciting and empowering experience. As a creative being, consciously connected to the Source from which everything happens, you are actively accessing great possibilities for your life. Here are the ways I guide visioning for my "Navigating Change" workshop participants, as well as practice it in my own life.

First, put yourself in a physical environment that feels beautiful and uplifting to you, whether you are taking a vision retreat, as described next, or you're in your own home or garden. Be alone, without any interruptions or emails, and turn off your phone. Choose a time when you're well rested and refreshed so you can fully attune to your vision with high energy.

Meditate on the Being Vision you created in Phase 3, and reflect on what is most important for you to bring into your life right now. Appreciate the road you've travelled thus far, the things you've accomplished that you are proud of, and the wisdom and courage and depth you have gathered through your life experiences.

Invite your own Higher Self, or Spirit, to lead you in the creation of your next vision. Get in touch with what is calling you to be expressed or created next in your life, that which would feel fulfilling and nourishing to you. When your vision becomes clear, write it down. Write spontaneously at first, without editing, in freely flowing words, as if you are channeling this vision from your own Higher Self, which, indeed, you are. State your vision in expansive, positive statements.

Write your vision in the present tense. "I *am* (living in a home that nurtures me, doing work I love with people I enjoy, travelling to inspiring places, in a healthy, fulfilling relationship," etc.), *not* "I *will be* doing this." Your subconscious mind takes your statements literally, and "I *will be* ..." tells your subconscious that you are not there now. Fill

*Let yourself be silently drawn by the pull of what you really love.*

≋☆ RUMI

yourself with the positive feelings and the internal knowing that yes, this vision statement is who you are *now*. The outside world of form simply hasn't caught up yet, but it will, and at the perfect time.

When you are finished, read your vision to yourself with great love, deep heart, and personal belief. As you do, feel yourself energetically aligning with it. Let the vision statement become part of who you know yourself to be and how you identify yourself. Let yourself be immersed in the enjoyable feelings of the vision before you even see it happening, and then allow the universe, the unified field of All that is, to bring you the perfect opportunities and invitations to enact your vision. And when these invitations from life show up, say yes! And act.

## Taking a Personal Vision Retreat

*Taking a vision retreat away from home gives you space and time to find your path with heart.* When a big life vision or new outer expression is calling you, your inner voice needs time and space to be heard and show you what trail to take next. If you are at this point in your life, consider taking a vision retreat. What would be the most inspiring vision retreat you could create for yourself that works with your current commitments?

Make space to hear your call by getting away from your everyday world. Taking a vision retreat can dramatically open your perception for what's possible in your life. Your vision retreat may be an overnight or a few days at an inn, at a retreat center, or camping. Take the kind of vision retreat that you feel drawn to and that works within your present lifestyle.

*Don't be satisfied with stories, how things have gone for others.*

*Unfold your own myth.*

≈✦ RUMI

Getting away expands us. Changing our environment bumps us out of our usual mindsets, aiding us in shifting old patterns that are holding us back. We move into different physical fields, landscapes, and rhythms. Gone are the attention-grabbing distractions of email, texts, phone calls, and television. We can find new answers and bigger truths about our lives when in fresh new places, either for a weekend of retreat or on a major soul pilgrimage. Flinging ourselves out of the nest of the known, we just may hatch the new soul-birds of ourselves.

*I went to the woods because I wished to live deliberately, to front only the essential faces of life, and see if I could not learn what it had to teach, and not, when I came to die, discover that I had not lived.*

⋙ HENRY DAVID THOREAU

### *Inspired Practice*

Plan a vision retreat for yourself. A couple of nights alone in a sacred space you love can bring great breakthroughs and insights about your life path. Envision a place where you can wander, walk in nature, journal or draw, listen to the stars, and be deeply present with yourself. Do you want friendly people around you at meals, perhaps at a monastery or retreat center? Do you want to sleep in a tent in the woods, surrounded by nature? Would you like to check into a wonderful inn alone, letting your vision experience unfold moment by moment? What kind of place and environment would serve you best and bring you the feeling of expansive openness to take your next steps into your new expression, your vision?

## A Vision Retreat Story

Many years ago, I drove the Pacific Coast Highway to Esalen Institute in Big Sur for a self-guided vision retreat. I'd been needing fresh new energy and direction in my professional life as a teacher and coach. I'd been questioning myself, feeling stuck in my teaching, wanting a breakthrough. I wondered if I should return to college for more training, but numerous forays into university and college programs had proven overly cerebral for my experiential, creative teaching and learning style. I wanted time to check in with myself undistracted, to write in my journal, draw, and feel, to be present with myself fully, engaging directly with whatever was brewing in me. I checked into my private room, soaked in the outdoor hot springs, and slept deeply, watched over by the stars outside my window.

The next morning, I set out early for the Art Barn, a magical art space out on the edge of Esalen's property that is usually open for anyone to drop in and create art. I set myself up at a picnic table facing the ocean, high on the Big Sur cliffs. Miraculously, I had the entire barn to myself. I had simple art supplies, a blank posterboard, a jar of hot coffee, a bottle of water, and a sun hat. I stepped into my inner Mystery to see what needed my attention.

I put my hand on the paper and began to draw without consciously directing what I was drawing. Over the next few hours, a map for my life emerged that showed me exactly where I've been, where I was at that moment in time, and where I was going. The brilliant wisdom of the inner guiding soul, or psyche, was guiding me. Although I am an artist and know how to draw, for this visioning exercise I just drew simple, childlike drawings to allow my inner images to come forth. I didn't plan a thing, and allowed one image to guide me to the next. (A collage of torn images from magazines that speak to you can also work well for this exploration.)

In the center of the white board I first drew a woman holding a large map. The map was filled with symbols she was in the process of deciphering. To her left was what she had left behind—cobwebs and dirt with hands grasping for her life, her love, herself. She stood before an arching gate with a purple bird on top of the gate. To her right, a golden doorway was being held open by smiling men and women, future mentors and friends, and new parts of herself, all welcoming her onto her new path. The path beyond the gate stretched up to the top of a shining, light-drenched mountain. I drew and painted spontaneously with simple colored pens, without thinking or planning, just seeing what needed to come forth from inside.

Facing the sparkling sunlight dancing off the ocean, with paints and drawing materials all around me, my hopes soared as I gazed at the results of my hours of drawing and painting. I felt inspiration for the path to come, the mentors waiting for me, the clarity of learning even more deeply what life is about and who I am. The painting completed something profound inside of me seeking my truth and direction.

I went to lunch and rested, then later returned to my table, taking out my big vision drawing. Next, I wrote in my journal about what each part of the drawing was saying to me. I wrote freely, without thinking or editing. My vision for the next steps in my life, my teaching, my personal study, and my world became clear to me as I wrote.

When I was done, I went to Nepenthe for dinner, a fantastic restaurant which rests like a big sea bird on the cliffs of Big Sur, hundreds of feet above the crashing surf. A soaring wooden sculpture of the mythical Phoenix bird greets visitors at the entrance. I felt my own Phoenix rising up that day, symbolized by this sculpture.

I had a breakthrough from my vision retreat. I felt a sense of freedom and empowerment I had not been able to find prior to my time away. I had clarity about my next steps to take. When I returned home, I designed a new workshop reflecting what I'd discovered, and my teaching went to a higher level.

# Commencement: Manifesting Your Vision

## Hearing the Guiding Voice of Spirit

There is a way to receive clear inner guidance for every question you have in your life, and that is by attuning to the wisdom of your own Higher Self. You cannot hear this voice when you're taking directions from the small self, who's always busy planning, strategizing, and thinking. These actions are all necessary for functioning in the world, but they come *after* receiving clear inner guidance, not at the outset of a new beginning. If you initiate any new beginning in your life by first figuring things out from the small self or ego mind, you are blocking your spiritual access to your biggest possibilities.

Your small self only knows how he or she used to do things. She operates in a limited field of her past beliefs and experiences of what used to work. She takes action from her historical strategies for accomplishing things. This is effective if you want to keep repeating what you used to

*As you go along in life, ask yourself, "Is this worthy of my soul?*

*Is this what I'm meant to be doing?"*

⧉ NIKOS KAZANTZAKIS

know and how you used to create things in your life. But, by doing this, you're actually blocking bigger possibilities that are awaiting you, and surrounding you all the time.

When you break out of your old, conditioned ways of responding to life, both psychologically and spiritually, you open up space to make great new choices guiding the way you live and think and be. Once you make that inspired decision, your small self, the advice-giving neighbor who loves to call up and offer her input, gets threatened. She wants you to live from her opinions and ideas. She may get on auto-dial for a while trying to sell you her version of how to create your life and how to move forward. When your small self is on the phone—and, rest assured, this happens with regularity for us all—gently but firmly say, "No, thank you." Then ask Spirit, or your own Higher Self, for guidance.

To support yourself in hearing this inner guidance, go to a quiet place in your home or in nature for meditation. Once you find yourself in a peaceful place of Being, attuned to your Higher Self, simply ask for the guidance you seek with an open mind and heart. Then be quiet and listen. Pay attention to the ideas, intuitions, and insights that come to you. Don't disregard them as too out of the box, or not sounding like what you used to know, or how you used to do things. If nothing comes in, be patient and trust the process.

The infinite has no timetable. It brings us opportunities, people, and solutions as we are aligned to receiving our greatest good. Our alignment to this good comes through Being, not through rushing around and doing. When you feel clear guidance, write it down in your journal. Allow the voice of your own inner wisdom to speak to you and show you what to do next.

*Start seeing everything as God, but keep it a secret.*

≈✵ HAFIZ

*The infinite has no timetable. It brings us opportunities, people, and solutions as we are aligned to receiving our greatest good.*

Once you have your inner guidance, act! *Now* is the time for making calls, writing the book, initiating the move, reaching out to someone, or expressing yourself in the ways you feel inspired to do. But let your planning and action also come from Spirit, guided from your Higher Self. Simply ask your Higher Self, "How should I take action from here? What should I do next?" Write down what you hear or sense to be the guidance. Do this intuitively and see what happens. Then move into action, guided by Being, inner knowing, and your own Higher Self.

Great possibilities and joyful outcomes are always available to us when we're consciously connected to the unified field, to Spirit, or the Source. Access to this field comes from letting our new vision for any part of our lives come from Being, not from forcing and thinking and trying to make things happen from the ego. The instant we realize we've gone off course and are moving from fear, not love, from pushing, not Being, we need to choose a higher thought to adjust our course. We acknowledge our passing emotional states with humor and humility, without any suppression or self-judgment, then simply shift back to our Being and our connection to our Higher Self. It's a little dance in which we are increasingly led by our Higher Self, and cut into less and less by our small self with its limiting agendas, fears, and judgments.

When we feel clear about our next steps, then we take them. It may be as simple as inviting a new friend to have lunch or as sweeping as a new career direction, a creative project you're embarking on, a relationship you are exploring, or a meaningful trip you want to take. Listen and follow.

## Align to Your Vision and the Universe Runs to Meet You

**Once you create your vision and clearly write it down with positive, expectant energy, the universe is already conspiring to assist you.** As long as your vision is aligned to your highest good and your Being, then it's coming to meet you.

Years ago I was meditating in my garden in Santa Fe. I could feel a new expression calling in my work as a teacher. I wanted to work with teenagers. I love teenagers, the feistier and smarter and edgier, the better. They remind me of me as a young woman, and that me desperately needed a mentor. I called my good friend Joel Feldman, a great life coach.

"I want to work with teenagers," I said. "I love them. I love the way they think and do everything and challenge everything."

"Well, what would you most like to do with teenagers?" Joel asked.

"I'd like to do experiential leadership retreats with teens. I want to help them step into their power and voice and greatness."

"Great idea!" Joel said. "How would you do that?"

I was energized when we hung up. On the spot, I got out my journal and wrote an impassioned vision statement about offering leadership retreats for teens. I felt enthusiastic and inspired. I had no idea how to make this happen; I just stayed with the vision and my positive, expectant feelings.

The next day, I attended a large garden party at the home of a neighbor. As I lunched on the patio, my attention was drawn beyond the guests to a redheaded woman in her forties serving us sandwiches and drinks on a silver tray. There was an aura about her, something special I picked up. I reached out to her on her break.

"Who *are* you?" I asked.

"I'm Myra Murphy Jacobs."

"Well, what are you doing here serving sandwiches?" I asked.

She smiled. "I assist the owner here a couple of days a week. I like her, and it pays the bills. But my real work, the work I've launched in the world, is that I am the Executive Director of SGLA, the Sustainable Global Leadership Alliance, a group that guides teenagers through an eight-week program in developing their leadership to serve the world. And what do you do?" she asked me.

"I am a leadership trainer for teenagers," I said, without skipping a beat.

"Wow, we have to get together. I have all my trainers lined up except for our leadership trainer. What are you doing tomorrow afternoon?" she asked.

"Meeting with you!" I said.

The next day, Myra and I spent three hours on my front porch sharing about our life paths. I didn't speak much about my leadership background or my philosophy for teaching leadership, and she didn't ask. At the end of our visit, she invited me to be the SGLA leadership trainer.

I led teen leadership retreats for several years at my One Spirit retreat center in Tesuque, New Mexico. I loved having teenagers all over my land, journaling on rocks in the river, brilliantly interpreting quantum physics and Taoist philosophies I'd pitch out to them, drumming and singing under the cottonwoods, and sharing their dreams for life. By allowing myself to hear my next vision coming in, name it, write it down, and believe I would be doing this wonderful work, the universe brought it in.

Certainly, not everything we wish for or envision happens this quickly, or even comes to pass. With self-reflection, we can usually see how some old fear or limiting belief we're carrying is getting in the way. Sometimes, with hindsight, we may realize a relationship, house, job, or situation we thought we really needed in order to be happy would not have been a vibrational match for us, nor brought us lasting fulfillment. These experiences invite us back into living from Being, the true Source of our happiness and fulfillment, and being led by Spirit. Often such disappointments eventually usher in higher possibilities for us, ones that are truly aligned to our greatest good.

## The Unplanted Field

*After we've readied our gardens, we have to plant our fields.* Just down the road from my former home in New Mexico was the perfect farming field in our rural village of Tesuque. It received full-tilt southern exposure sunlight all day. It was always freshly disked, the sun-warmed earth waiting to be planted.

I stopped shortly after moving to the area to meet the old man I saw out there each day in a pith helmet and impeccable work coveralls, readying his field. Mr. Garcia strode over to greet me at his fence. "Hi, I'm your neighbor Christine. What a beautiful field this is," I said.

"Yes, it's good soil. I've been working it for years now," he smiled. His neat rows of irrigation sprinklers stood at attention in the glistening, weedless, perfectly ploughed rows.

"What are you going to plant?" I asked.

He tensed up suddenly. "I don't know yet! I'm just getting it ready!" he said testily.

"Of course you are!" I said, backing away from what seemed to be a hot topic for him. I invited him to come visit for tea one day, and we said goodbye.

The years passed, and each day I drove by Mr. Garcia's field. I never saw a crop out there, a garden, vegetables, roses, orchard, nothing. Spring, summer, fall, Mr. Garcia was always out there ploughing, disking, irrigating; but the fields stood empty, as if calling him: "We're ready! Plant something!" But no. I imagined him at the kitchen table of his villa, sipping his morning coffee, year after year, planning the marvelous things he is going to plant . . . someday.

Don't let your life be a perpetual vision quest that never gets anywhere. If there's a polar opposite to the error of rushing too fast to create a new vision for your life before you're internally ready, it's not taking clear, decisive, concrete action when you *are* ready to enact your dreams and visions. You have to actually move into gear and bring those dreams and beautiful instinctual urges into worldly action.

*First say to yourself what you would be; and then do what you have to do.*

≋ EPICTETUS

---

### Inspired Practice

What unplanted fields do you have inside you? Make a list of the steps you need to take to get your field of dreams planted. Then take action. Call the person you dream about calling, do the research to step forward with your vision, make the contact you think may help you move toward your new expression. Ask for the support you need to move on your way, and get going. It's time to plant your field.

## Each Step Illuminates the Next One

*There is no way. You make the way by walking out on it.*

≋✷ ANTONIO MACHADO

**As you walk through your life and enact your vision, you cannot see the whole path at once.** As you take one step on your path, it lights up, and you see, "Oh, here I am on this step. Now I see the next step to take." Then that step lights up and you have an intuition, "I think I'll call this person. Wouldn't it be great to take this class, or invite this conversation, or go to this place?" Each step illuminates the next one. If you never take the first step, you won't see the next ones waiting just beyond it.

Let your dreaming become doing. How? By taking small steps every day toward your vision. Begin with the steps you can take right now so you can live your dreams in small ways, at least to begin. You may not become a Metropolitan Opera star if you're beginning to sing later in life, but you *can* take voice lessons and learn to read some music. You can then be part of people singing together in fun, informal ways. You can then join a community choir. You can take steps to start living your vision right now.

As you take steps to follow your dreams and callings, each step changes you. You see new vistas appear that were not clear to you at the outset. Your path unfolds itself, one step at a time.

We can never know the whole path, the whole journey. That is a grace, and that is wonderful. It keeps us fresh and trusting the Mystery, listening to our inner guidance. As you follow your vision, who you are can shine forth. You find the steps to take, one at a time, to allow your gifts, your love, and your talents to shine forth to bless you and, therefore, the whole world.

—————————— ᘜ ——————————

## *Inspired Practice*

Make a list of steps you can take to start living your vision. Include simple ones: go to a lecture, walk with a friend, do what you love, take someone to lunch who's in the field you want to explore. Make a call, take a class, commit to an activity. Now write your commitments of small steps into your calendar and begin to pursue taking movement doing what you love.

—————————— ᘜ ——————————

## Risk Taking: Going Just Beyond Your Edge

**We have to take risks in life to live our dreams.** I love the story of author and teacher Sark, and how she took a wild risk when totally broke to follow her vision of having an artistic life. In 1989, Sark was seeking a studio living space in San Francisco, a notoriously expensive real estate market. She was getting by through bartering and trading, and was down to one dollar when she saw a sign advertising a "magic cottage" for rent. Having no funds didn't stop her, and she called the number on the sign. "Sorry, it's been rented," she was told.

"That's ok, because you'll be renting it to me," she replied. She went to see the cottage, a 180-square-foot tool shed converted into a small studio with a teeny bathroom. It was renting for $1,300 a month. She wrote a check on Friday for the rent, then set about figuring out how to get $1,299 to cover the check by Monday morning.

*Come to the edge, he*
*said,*
*They said: We are afraid.*
*Come to the edge, he*
*said.*
*They went to the edge.*
*He pushed them . . . and*
*they flew.*

 GUILLAUME
APOLLINAIRE

This is an important point that divides inspired, action-taking visionaries from the herd: taking a risk and believing, and knowing, that you are going to manifest the means to back up your vision. But here's the tricky part: if you are in fear, and don't believe things will work out, then they won't. Your fear will disable your good intentions. You need to honestly know your personal ability to take risks, without any shame or guilt, so that you know what you can comfortably tackle in life.

That weekend Sark sold most of her possessions and borrowed the rental balance from her brother. She was on her way. Shortly after moving into the magic cottage with her cat, Jupiter, she drew a piece in rainbow colors in her journal titled, "How to be an Artist," a manifesto for living life playfully and dreamily. A visiting friend saw the piece and said, "This would make a great poster." Days later, Sark took it to a business that sold posters. Within days they had 250 orders.

She began furiously hand-making copies of her poster until she'd made and sold 1,100 copies, then finally took it to a print shop. "How to Be an Artist" is now a worldwide seller. Books on creative living followed, workshops ensued, speaking engagements came after, and today Sark is a success story, now living in the main house and still working out of the magic cottage, having purchased the entire property following her whirlwind success.

Sark didn't move into her cottage thinking, "I'll go out on a limb because I'll become rich and famous here." I imagine she moved in thinking, "I will love living here and making art. The universe will take care of the rest." When we are living aligned to our dreams with faith in the benevolence of the universe, our needs are taken care of, not always in the way we hope they will be, but often in much better ways. Even if Sark had not become a professional success, in my view her life would be a grand success because she lived her vision and creative calling to the hilt.

You don't need to take the level of big, wild risk that Sark did to move toward your dreams, but you do have to take some level of risk to start to live from a bigger vision. Without some risk, you remain static in your old way of living your life. However, you have to know and respect your own capacity to take risks. Don't take a risk that puts you in a position where you panic, your fear becomes overwhelming, and you run back to the security of the known. Choose risks that move you just beyond your envelope of inner security, just enough so that you're stretching, but not so much that you snap. If you move too far out of your comfort zone, you could actually regress even further back than you were before you started, like a rubber band that has been overstretched and snaps back.

## Inspired Practice

*Ask yourself:* In my work, in my body, in my relationships, in my creative development, what is a risk I am wanting to take right now? Am I willing to take skiing lessons and be a rank beginner on the bunny slope? Am I willing to plan that trip to Brazil, or sign up for a dance class, history class, or choir? Will I join a creative writing class to pursue my love of literature? Am I willing to turn my dreams into some concrete actions, and do them now? What small risks can I take now to move me toward living my big vision, instead of just dreaming about it?

## Making Mistakes and Embracing Failure

*Make new mistakes. Make glorious, amazing mistakes. Make mistakes nobody's ever made before.*

≈✷ NEIL GAIMON

*Mistake-makers are visionaries who put themselves out on the line and try new things in order to follow their stars.*

**To take risks to follow your vision, learn to embrace apparent failure and mistakes as gifts.** What you may label as failure can be a marvelous opportunity to learn what didn't work and to reset your course. Each small risk you take requires facing the possibility of failure, whether large or small. If you take a class in your calling, you might feel scared or not do well at first. It may take a few forays into a new field to locate a teacher or group with whom you feel comfortable and inspired. Keep at it and give yourself room to experiment. If you call a mentor for a visit to receive guidance, she may be too busy to see you. Call the next person on your list.

Mistake-makers are visionaries who put themselves out on the line and try new things in order to follow their stars. No one becomes great by shrinking back and waiting around to see what everyone else is doing, or what everyone else will approve of. Be yourself and create your vision in your own utterly unique way. Get started on your vision. Make some great mistakes. Learn from so-called failures. Regard them all as footsteps on your path to living from your own unique vision, the outer expression of your Being.

A coaching client of mine launched her latest novel into the world, a big departure from the style in which she'd previously written. She wanted to break new ground and attempt something aligned to a new sense of Being she'd found in herself. Her new novel had a mixed review in the *New York Times*, acknowledging both strengths and weaknesses in the work. When I saw the review, I wondered how she'd feel about it. But when we had our next phone coaching session, she was ebullient about the *Times* review. "I had to sit with this for a while," she shared. "Then I realized what a tremendous gift this was to me." I listened in wonderment. "The smartest and best literary reviewers in the world just gave me free advice about how to improve my writing. Fantastic!" No wonder this woman is a huge success in her craft.

When disappointment happens as you're creating a new vision for a part of your life, it's a chance to forge an even better path for yourself, and an opportunity to learn something valuable. If you pay attention and learn from what you define as failure, your learning will help you move on in a new direction.

Our mistakes and failures are indicators that there is a more joyful, creative, vibrationally aligned approach awaiting us. What might that be? What's possible?

## Living Your Calling versus Making a Living

**Great people have often begun their enterprises humbly, but with much love and enthusiasm.** Their positive energy and deeply held intentions for what they want nurture their work. But the ego's pressure to hurry up and be rich and famous by doing what we love can stifle the life out of our dreams before they even begin blossoming.

A well-travelled business trainer and consultant once came for a coaching session. She shared that she made thousands of dollars for a day's training with corporate executives, but was "bored out of my mind" with her work. She was stuck in the success trap, being financially successful at doing something she didn't like.

She sat on my white cotton office couch, a lit candle between us, gazing at me. "I want to be *you*. I want to do what *you're* doing—lead spiritual, experiential growth

*They say just do what you love and the money will follow. I don't think so.*

≋ JOAN SOTKIN,
PROSPERITY COACH

workshops—but I want to make a lot of money doing it."
I have heard this before. It always makes me think of the
Hindu story of the monkey with his paw stuck inside the hole
in the coconut. He wants to eat the meat, but cannot with-
draw his paw to get it without letting go of the meat itself.
He remains stuck in a comedic trap—hungry for the juicy
coconut meat—but unable to let go and free himself.

I saw this talented, gifted woman mixing up her heartfelt desire to teach spirituality with her ego's desire to sustain status and wealth in a professional world she actually
cared little about. Her Being Vision was not aligned to her
work, and her work was so demanding there was no time
left to be creative and follow her dreams of spiritual teaching on the side. Her thirst to follow her spiritual calling to
teach was strong. She was a brilliant woman caught with
her hand clenched in the fame-and-money coconut. She
could have easily sustained her career, reduced her hours,
and begun leading spiritual groups as a fulfilling expression
in her life part-time, even one evening a week. This wasn't
appealing to her. It had to be all or nothing. We did one
session and then I didn't hear from her.

Two years later we met at a concert. I asked her how
she was. She rolled her eyes. "Christine, I'm still travelling
all the time doing my corporate work. I still haven't started
teaching spiritual classes," she said, almost apologetically.
She ticked off the cities she'd trained in over the past few
months. I could see her exhaustion. "One of these days I'll
be in town long enough to take one of your workshops," she
said. I said I would welcome her.

One of the major traps that keep people from following
their call and living the lives they want is the ego's pressure
to make money and be a huge success immediately, before
they have taken small steps to nurture their visions. Often

such people never even get started with a class, a group, a workshop, or retreat aligned to their callings because they can't immediately become accomplished and important or fulfill their concepts of money and fame. This is a tragic and unnecessary loss of fulfillment and joy.

Sometimes a vision becomes a source of financial success, and sometimes it thrives best when separated from the way you earn income. Give your dreams breathing space. Don't pressure them to pull in big dollars before they have a chance to develop. I often encourage clients creating a new life vision to initially keep their current work for steady income, creatively reducing hours if possible, while finding innovative ways to develop and grow their calling, so they have the pure joy of doing what they love. Whether or not their calling is one day lucrative, it will always be a source of personal fulfillment.

*Look at every path closely and deliberately . . .*
*Then ask yourself one question:*
*Does this path have a heart?*

≈✷ CARLOS CASTENEDA

## Ask and the Door Will Open

A major career shift in my life twenty years ago illustrates the importance of following the inner voice of intuition and Spirit's guidance that comes to us. I was ready to let go of my co-ownership of the corporate training company I had founded ten years earlier with my first husband, Paul. My soul was calling for more free time to paint, write, and live creatively. We were in a dry period contractually and our savings had dwindled to nearly nothing. I had no nest egg to fall back on. In spite of this, I knew in my heart that I had to follow the call to live my creative life, a calling I'd had all my life.

We hired a mediator to navigate the difficult terrain of being a couple separating out a co-owned business. I had to

*Ask, and it shall be given; knock, and the door will open.*

≈✷ CHRIST

take the risk of standing on my own feet financially without any foreseeable job.

The morning following our final signing of papers ending my co-ownership of our company, I went to my altar and lit a candle. I vividly remember that pivotal morning of my life. Sitting there on my blue velvet meditation cushion, I knew I had done the right thing for my soul, but I had absolutely no idea how I would manifest income. I gazed out over the summer maple trees surrounding our home, and called on Spirit for guidance. I offered my need for meaningful work in prayer, and then emptied my mind and meditated, dropping below anxiety and control to the peace of God, so familiar from years of spiritual practice.

Out of the blue, an intuitive message came, clear as a bell: "Go call Mike. Call right now." Mike was the director of a Conscious Leadership Center which Kripalu Center had founded, situated in a large Victorian mansion on a lake nearby. The center was well underway with a large team of talented professionals, and there was no need for more staff that I was aware of. It would have been so easy to brush off my guidance as ridiculous, but here it was: call Mike.

I stood up and walked across the hall from my meditation room to my office, and dialed Mike.

"I was just thinking about you," I said. "I'd love to chat with you sometime about the Leadership Center and hear how everything is going."

"What are you doing now?" he asked. "Would you like to come over and take a walk?"

"Yes!" I said.

Soon Mike and I were strolling the center's magnificent grounds, having a friendly conversation about the center's growth and development. He invited me to take part in the upcoming inaugural training as the center's guest, to gather my feedback afterward on improving the training. I said sure, that would be fun.

Following the program and my input, Mike offered me a job as a leadership trainer, redesigning the curriculum using the excellent core leadership model the team had created, and then co-leading the retreat. Within several months, Mike changed careers, and invited me to be the new center director.

From having no plan on the horizon, but following my vision, asking for guidance, listening, and then acting on the guidance that showed up, I now had meaningful, heart-centered work. I was working collaboratively with wonderful people I loved being around. My office was the elegant master suite of a former Vanderbilt mansion. I was able to set up my own schedule and create space for painting. I served some wonderful business owners and visionary, caring executives whom I was honored to support. I paid my bills and saved money.

After a year and a half, Kripalu restructured and ceased all outsourced projects, closing the Leadership Center in the process. Shortly after this, Paul and I amicably decided to end our marriage. I followed a years-long dream of moving to Santa Fe to become a fulltime painter. I was forty-five, free of debt, owned my car, and had saved a modest amount that allowed me to begin my new life as an artist. I painted for seven years and fulfilled my dream of being a painter. Then I returned to my lifetime calling as a spiritual and personal growth teacher, still painting today when time allows.

Ask, and the door will open. And when it opens, stand up and walk through it.

# SECTION 4

# The Journey Continues

## The Circle of Change

**E**very new beginning contains the invisible seeds of its own **ending, and every ending opens space for something new to be born.** The circle of change is always with us. We are never finished with the journey of change, but are engaged in different phases of change at different points in our lives.

A friend of mine once took a vision quest during a turbulent time in his life. He and his wife had separated and were deciding whether to remain married or not. His mother had passed on, leaving him in deep grief and loss. His once-flourishing business was floundering. He needed to get away and go into nature to find healing and clarity, a new direction, and a new vision.

He decided to do a retreat on the wild Na Pali coast of Kauai. The Na Pali trail is rugged, just a footpath carved into the steep side of high cliffs overlooking the Pacific. On the two-day hike to his campsite, at a certain point on the trail, he came across the body of a wild goat who had just died right on the trail. He blessed the goat, and continued on.

*We shall not cease from exploration,*
*And the end of all our exploring*
*Will be to arrive where we started*
*And know the place for the first time.*

≋✶ T.S. ELIOT

He hiked into the Kalalau valley in the Na Pali to camp and do his vision retreat. He found answers and had a major breakthrough about his marriage, his work, and himself. After five days, he felt clear and free. It was time to hike back out. Then a stunning event happened. At the exact spot on the trail where he had encountered the dead goat when hiking in, there was now a female goat giving birth, right before his eyes. He wept at the perfect message from life mirroring his own endings, the deaths of what had been, and heralding a new birth, a new beginning.

The parts of our lives that once resonated so well with who we were when we created them have to eventually shift or be released for the new forms to be born. Although all things must change to vibrate with who we've become, not every outer form needs to shift. You may already have a marriage, a profession, a lifestyle, or a home that you deeply love and thrive in. If this is true for you, then the way you *inhabit* those forms will call for change over time. This is a wonderful process, as it keeps your life, your work, your relationships, and your way of Being fresh, always supporting your growth and true fulfillment.

We're here to have joy and to grow in equal measure. Part of the magnificence of being human is the pleasure and delight of falling in love, having great friends, manifesting our true work, and creating homes that are sanctuaries and nests for us, whether simple or palatial. If we use what we do and create in our lives for our higher purpose of growth, then every experience, every ending, and every new beginning is always just right. Everything we experience is a gift that is perfectly calibrated to help us evolve and live more deeply from our truth, our own Higher Self, or God within us.

## Shine Your Life

*When you make loving others the story of your life, there's never a final chapter.*

≈✷ OPRAH

**As a limitless being and expression of the Divine, you have within you, right now, everything you need to begin to live your vision.** Each moment gives you a fresh chance to choose what brings you fulfillment from the inside, your Being, to the outside, your doing, your expression in your life. Connected to the Source, freed of past wounds and beliefs through your intentional work to heal yourself, trusting in the Mystery of All that is, knowing who you are in your Being, and focusing clearly on the path you want to take, you become a blazing star in your own existence. You become filled-full in the experience of being alive in your own life. You shine your light into the lives of those whose paths touch yours.

This book has been a journey from endings to new beginnings, from the human to the Divine. It has guided you in letting go of outgrown forms and ways of being. It has held your hand through the times of the Mystery, not-seeing what's next, not-knowing how to proceed, and learning the rare gift of being right here in the moment. It has introduced you to your own phoenix, a new way of being alive rising up within you. Finally, it has reminded you of the spiritual, unified field where you live, containing infinite support, guidance, and possibilities. It's given you a map for initiating visionary beginnings in your life, and tools for allowing them to flourish.

This book is ended, and your new life going forward has begun. May you travel with love for all that comes your way, and use every experience to remember who you are, to deepen yourself in ways that fulfill you, and to bring light to your own life and to the world. Thank you for walking the path of navigating change with me.

*I wish you courage, faith, and happiness*
*as you walk your path with heart.*

# ACKNOWLEDGEMENTS

I'm deeply grateful to all those who have believed in me as a teacher and writer, making this book possible. Your love, encouragement and energy live in these pages.

A deep bow to my husband, Kenn Holsten, my resident wise man, brilliant editor, stalwart supporter, and cheerleader throughout the process of my writing and refining this book over many years. Thank you for your dedicated involvement, your insightful comments, and your love, apparent in every page.

To my friends who enthusiastically encouraged me to write this book, especially Kate and Joel Feldman, Linda Earls, Betsy Warren, and Paul Deslauriers.

My talented book designer, Michael Rohani, brought form and beauty to my words with his inspired star/compass cover and his page designs for this book.

To all of the loving, courageous and wonderful people who have taken my "Navigating Change" workshops, and who kept asking for this book.

Finally, loving thanks to my very special clients, students, and friends whose stories appear in these pages. May your own profound life navigations inspire and help others to find their way home.

# ABOUT THE AUTHOR

**C**hristine Warren is a 40-year national presenter of transformational workshops and a life coach and counselor, consultant, and speaker. A founding member of Kripalu Center, she has led transformational workshops at Esalen Institute, Omega Institute, Rowe Center, Kripalu Center, 1440 Multiversity, Lesley College, Long Island University and many other venues.

Her next book, *Beyond Change: A Guide to Spiritual Awakenings in Life Transitions*, will be published in the spring of 2018.

Christine was the director of Kripalu's Foxhollow Leadership Center and co-director of New Resources for Growth, a corporate training company. She is a motivational speaker and has led executive retreats in conscious leadership, vision, and team-building for the executive teams of over 50 leading corporations and for the Young Presidents' Organizations.

Christine has a private practice as a life coach, counselor, and Personal Retreat guide. She divides her time between Maui and Santa Fe. Information on her private sessions, life coaching and workshops can be found at *www.ChristineWarrenWorkshops.com.*

CPSIA information can be obtained
at www.ICGtesting.com
Printed in the USA
FSOW04n1158021017
39408FS